Understanding, Measuring, and Improving Overall Equipment Effectiveness

How to Use OEE to Drive Significant
Process Improvement

Understanding, Measuring, and Improving Overall Equipment Effectiveness

How to Use OEE to Drive Significant Process Improvement

Ross Kenneth Kennedy

CRC Press
Taylor & Francis Group
Boca Raton London New York

CRC Press is an imprint of the
Taylor & Francis Group, an **informa** business

CRC Press
Taylor & Francis Group
6000 Broken Sound Parkway NW, Suite 300
Boca Raton, FL 33487-2742

© 2018 by Taylor & Francis Group, LLC
CRC Press is an imprint of Taylor & Francis Group, an Informa business

No claim to original U.S. Government works

Printed on acid-free paper

International Standard Book Number-13: 978-1-138-05420-2 (Paperback)

Visit the Taylor & Francis Web site at
http://www.taylorandfrancis.com

and the CRC Press Web site at
http://www.crcpress.com

Contents

Chapter 1

Understanding OEE

The concept of Overall Equipment Effectiveness (OEE) was first written about in 1989 from a book called *TPM Development Program: Implementing Total Productive Maintenance* edited by Seiichi Nakajima from the Japan Institute of Plant Maintenance. This was translated from the Japanese book *TPM tenkai* published in 1982.

Before OEE, people monitored equipment performance through Availability or Downtime. This was fine until it was realized that you could have the same downtime for the same piece of equipment over different timeframes yet get a different output.

For example, if a line's performance is measured over 100 hours and during this time it has one breakdown for 10 hours, Availability will be 90% and Downtime will be 10%. If the same line over another 100 hours had 10 breakdowns of 1 hour duration (total of 10 hours), then Availability would still be 90% and Downtime would be 10% (Figure 1.1).

However, when comparing output, in the majority of cases, the first situation of only one breakdown will produce significantly more output than the situation of 10 breakdowns. The logic is quite simple. Every time your plant stops unexpectedly, there is a high probability you will have some form of quality loss such as scrap or rework. Also, when you start back up again, there is a high probability that there will be a speed loss as you ramp the plant back up to full speed.

Hence, there was a need to create a measure that would reflect all losses that can affect the capacity to produce perfect, or within-specification, output first up. Ideally, the measure could also be used for prioritizing improvement activities while bringing everyone together to improve, as everyone would benefit from its improvement.

This is why OEE was developed. It was the first time you could measure how effective your equipment was at producing good output, recognizing that equipment is only effective if it is available when required, running at the ideal speed, and producing perfect or within-specification output.

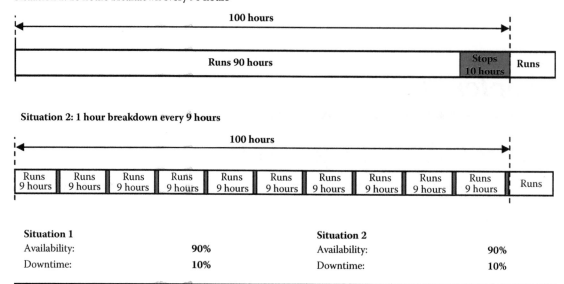

Figure 1.1   Limitations of downtime as a measure.

Nakajima wrote: Effectiveness can be measured using the following formula:

Overall Equipment Effectiveness = Availability × Performance rate × Quality rate

with the 6 Big Losses affecting OEE listed as follows:

Availability	Performance Rate	Quality Rate
• Breakdown losses • Setup and adjustment losses	• Idling and minor stoppage losses • Reduced speed losses	• Quality defect and rework losses • Start-up (yield) losses

In more recent literature, the OEE loss model has been expanded to include a further loss, Planned Downtime under Availability, creating 7 Losses (Figure 1.2).

The aim of the **7 Losses** is to capture all possible losses that could be improved operationally including such **Planned Downtime** as meal breaks, regular maintenance periods, start of shift, toolbox meetings, and so on.

Responsibility and Accountability for OEE

To understand who should be responsible and accountable for OEE, we have found it helpful to first identify some of the activities that may need to be addressed to eliminate or minimize the losses. For example:

■ Detect and Predict Deterioration
■ Establish Repair Methods

■ Restore Deterioration
■ Maintain Operating Standards
■ Maintain Basic Equipment Conditions
■ Prevent Incorrect Operation
■ Prevent Repair Errors
■ Improve Design Weaknesses

Then, ask the question: who should be involved in carrying out these activities?

The answer becomes obvious in that OEE Improvement involves all departments including the following: Production, Maintenance, Engineering, Quality, HR/Training, Procurement, and Planning and Scheduling.

However, one department needs to take full ***responsibility*** for the cost-effective performance of their plant and equipment and be ***accountable*** for the OEE.

If we think about our car, it is the way we drive it, the environment we keep it in, the frequency we get it serviced, and, most importantly, the timeliness we respond to any little problems we may encounter that has the biggest impact on the overall running cost and resale value of our car.

Production Plant and Equipment is no different. The way we operate it, the condition we keep it in, the frequency we allow maintenance to do their servicing, and the way we identify and respond to small problems before they become big problems all contribute significantly to the plant performance and the maintenance costs.

That is why the Production department must take full responsibility and accountability for OEE, recognizing they can't achieve best practice without every other department's support.

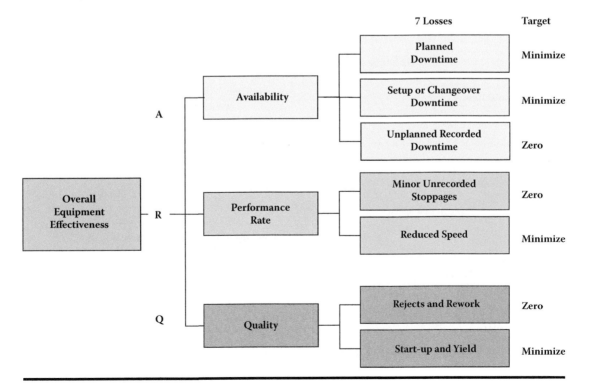

Figure 1.2   OEE Model.

Calculating OEE

OEE can be calculated either by using Equations or by using the Time Loss or Unit Loss model. Both give the same answer if done correctly.

Using Equations

There is a separate equation for Availability, Performance Rate, and Quality as outlined in Figure 1.3, which are normally expressed as a percentage. By multiplying the three percentages together, you come up with a percentage OEE.

These equations can also be simplified by crossing out common numerators (top of the line) and denominators (bottom of the line) to generate what we call a High-Level OEE equation.

By crossing out Actual Speed, Processed Amount, and Reported Production Time (Available Time – All Recorded Downtime), you are left with the simple High-Level OEE equation:

$$\textbf{Good Output Produced/(Available Time} \times \textbf{Ideal Speed)}$$

This is a very simple and easy way to calculate OEE and hence should be done regularly (hourly, daily, weekly) and graphed on a run chart for everyone to monitor. However, this approach does not highlight where the losses come from; hence, Sampling and Continuous Recording are also required to identify where best to focus improvement activities.

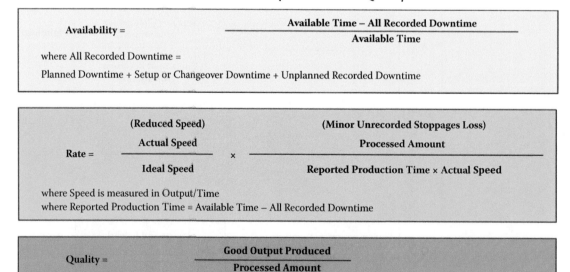

Figure 1.3   Calculating OEE using Equations.

Using the Time Loss or the Unit Loss Model

The Time Loss or Unit Loss model allows you to take data from Continuous Recording sheets or loss data collection systems and identify the time or unit magnitude of each of the losses to allow Pareto charts to be created to focus improvement activities (Figures 1.4 and 1.5). This can also be complemented with data collected during observations to pick up on the reasons for any minor unrecorded stoppages.

What Is Best Practice OEE?

Traditional thinking has often identified best practice OEE in a discrete manufacturing plant as 85% based on the notion of 90% Availability × 95% Rate × 99% Quality. The 90% Availability recognizes that there will be losses from Setup or Changeover downtime and, as a consequence of this, also have some speed loss associated with starting up again. In continuous process industries that don't have setup or changeover downtime, the best practice OEE is often stated as 95% based on 98% Availability × 98% Rate × 99% Quality.

Our learning has been that these numbers can be quite ridiculous at many sites and as such best practice OEE targets should be based on actual business requirements for each production line or area. For example, at one site, they had a high-speed multistage six-color printing line for creating decorated sheets of metal used for making aerosol cans. To ensure the perfect quality of printing, it could take up to 3.5 hours to change over the line to a new product and run sufficient samples

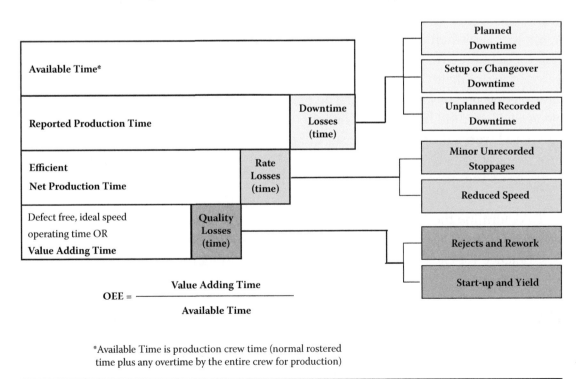

$$OEE = \frac{Value\ Adding\ Time}{Available\ Time}$$

*Available Time is production crew time (normal rostered time plus any overtime by the entire crew for production)

Figure 1.4   Calculating OEE using Time Loss.

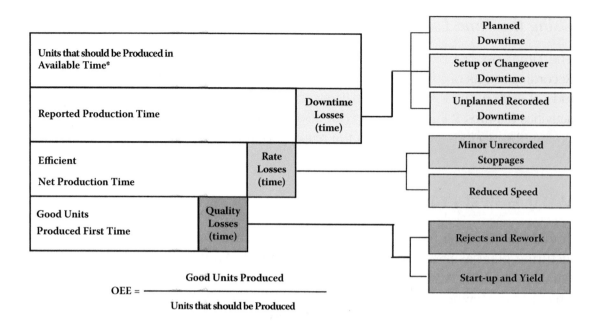

Figure 1.5 Calculating OEE using Unit Loss.

to verify the correct quality of printing. Because of the small market in Australia requiring small batch sizes and the very high speed of the line when it was running, the actual run time of the line was often only 30 minutes. If all went perfectly and there was no other downtime, then an OEE of 12.5% was best practice for that line. At another site where they were running a can line for a food product, the manager thought the line was going very good at 82% OEE; however, when we took a close look of their operational requirements, they only ran the line for 8 hours a day, making one product per day. The crew was manned so there were relief people available for the breaks (ran continuously for the 8 hours). The line was prepared and warmed up before the start of the shift and two people would stay back at the end of the shift to clean up the line. Hence, with no Planned Downtime or Setup or Changeover downtime, their OEE performance should have been closer to 98% rather than the traditional target of 85% being used by the manager.

To determine the best practice OEE target for each production line or area, you need to look at each of the 7 Losses and then list out your assumptions for best practice for each loss based on business requirements.

The Need to Understand and Monitor the Elements of OEE

Care needs to be taken when monitoring OEE performance as often some elements of OEE have a bigger impact on the bottom line than others. For example, we could have two situations where OEE is 85%:

Situation 1:

$$A = 90\% \times R = 95\% \times Q = 99\%, \text{ giving an OEE of 85\%.}$$

Situation 2:

$$A = 99\% \times R = 95\% \times Q = 90\%, \text{ giving an OEE of 85\%.}$$

Both situations provide an 85% OEE; however, in situation 2, a Quality of 90% could mean scrapping or reworking 10% of your raw materials, resulting in a possible expensive loss, compared to situation 1 where you are only scrapping or reworking 1% of your raw materials.

Why Is OEE Often Measured Incorrectly?

Speed Loss is a good starting point. This is the loss that a lot of people misunderstand and hence get very wrong, resulting in overinflated OEE performance.

Nakajima explained Speed Loss by stating: "Bring actual operation speed up to design speed; then make improvement to surpass design speed." To support this thinking, he uses the term Ideal Speed or Theoretical Speed for production lines and Ideal Cycle Time for component making machines.

In further publications from the Japan Institute of Plant Maintenance (e.g., *TPM in Process Industries* edited by Tokutaro Suzuki), we have found reference to Standard Rate; however, when looked at closely, "the standard production rate is equivalent to a plant's design capacity and is the intrinsic (inherent or real) capacity of a particular plant."

So, rather than identifying the Ideal (or theoretical) Speed of a line, a lot of companies and consultants to that matter use standard or budgeted speed taken from the production planning department for their calculations rather than recognizing that the aim of OEE is to assist sites to achieve world class performance rather than support average or standard performance.

The key learning about Speed or Rate for the OEE calculation has been as follows:

> ***Do not confuse ideal speed (designed to assist improvement)
> with rate used for costing or scheduling.***

For example, when scheduling, you need a rate to allow the production planner to make realistic promise commitments to customers. This is often referred to as budget rate, standard rate, or sometimes master production schedule rate. This rate has allowances built in for losses such as setup time, labor inefficiencies, past poor practices, and so on to ensure promises to customers will be achieved (e.g., demonstrated rate).

We have seen many examples where the best demonstrated rate (e.g., best five shifts for the year) has been initially used only to cause heartache when the figure significantly improves, resulting in performance rates of above 100% or adjustments to the best demonstrated rate such that the OEE drops. This can be even more detrimental when there is some incentive linked to OEE performance (another bad practice by companies we come across).

What Should Be the Purpose of OEE?

> OEE should be seen and used as a "driver" for improvement, not as a performance measure to be compared or benchmarked between equipment and sites.

It can also provide everyone with a simple indicator to monitor the amount of ongoing continuous improvement time that can be allocated each week to support Production Area Based Team improvement activities such as regular Clean for Inspections through Operator Equipment Management or Autonomous Maintenance.

STRIVING FOR PERFECT EQUIPMENT PERFORMANCE

When a site commences, the TPM or Total Productive Maintenance journey to Perfect Equipment Performance we recommend starting with several Cross-functional Improvement Teams focused on the critical bottleneck lines. Each Cross-functional Team over a period of 3–4 months, meeting weekly for one and a half hours, would first baseline current OEE performance, understand all the variables that could influence OEE, and then conduct detailed OEE Analysis using High-Level OEE, Continuous Recorded Data from production sheets or monitoring system, and, most importantly, several OEE observations.

Once an Ideal Vision for their critical bottleneck line is established and the reasons for the gap to the baseline OEE are understood, each team would initiate sufficient approved improvements to lift OEE by at least 15%. Once sufficient OEE gain has been achieved, Production Area Based Team improvement activity involving all shifts could commence recognizing, where practical, some of the OEE gain will need to be allocated to allow the production line to stop for regular improvement activities, which typically involve improving the work area using 5S principles and then regular Clean for Inspections through the 7 Steps of Operator Equipment Management or Autonomous Maintenance to find equipment defects and problems at the earliest possible time.

This, along with further targeted Cross-functional Improvement Team activity, will take the line performance to best practice. Meanwhile, an agreed OEE target becomes a key monitoring tool for all on the line or responsible for the line, to determine whether the Production Area Based Team improvement activities can be conducted each week.

OEE as a "Driver" for Improvement

We have found that OEE performance is very dependent on business needs. As such, a production line at one site might have a totally different OEE performance to an identical production line at another site, yet both production lines could be performing to "best practice."

Let us explain this using just one of the 7 Losses outlined in the OEE Model (this thinking can be applied to all the losses):

Setup or Changeover Downtime: This is normally defined as the time between last good output produced to the next required good output produced at the agreed target speed. If you wish to compare or benchmark OEE between lines, then you need to ensure that the lines being compared have exactly the same number of setups or changeovers and the same run lengths (amount produced between setups or batch size). Unless you have a dedicated line (no setups) that runs the same amount of time (e.g., 8 hours a day, 5 days a week so that there are equal start-ups, etc.), then the OEE performance will be different no matter how good the crew is running the line.

As a "driver" for Improvement, the definition for OEE should have a 100% correlation to the good output produced from your line or plant. In other words, if OEE increases by 10%, then you should be making 10% more good output or making the same amount of good output within 10% less time, hence the need for the OEE definition to include all the 7 Losses.

By having this 100% correlation, the OEE measure can be used to make decisions to support ongoing continuous improvement time for Production Area Based Teams. By this, we mean if OEE performance drops, then there is the risk that the required output for the week may not be achieved, in which case, stopping the line for the weekly Clean for Inspection to find equipment defects or sources for poor quality may need to be deferred so that customer commitments are achieved. If this does occur (deferment or cancellation of the Production Area Based Team improvement activities for the week owing to the need to achieve the Production Plan for the week), then you would expect the team would conduct a root cause analysis as to why it occurred and initiate corrective actions so it does not occur again for that same reason.

If You Shouldn't Benchmark OEE, What Should It Be Used For?

As mentioned earlier, OEE is an "improvement driver." As such, you need to determine what your best practice target is for each of the 7 Losses. This can also be broken down into sections of your line (e.g., filler, labeler, packer, palletizer, etc.). The tool we have developed to assist this important process is the OEE Loss Analysis Spreadsheet (covered in Chapter 5), which typically involves a 1st-Level and 2nd-Level Analysis of the 7 Losses of OEE and the sections where the losses are occurring.

The OEE Loss Analysis has several purposes and is normally conducted every 12 months for each Production Area (e.g., a bottling line) to allow reflection on previous predictions, and map out the plan for the next 12 months supported by a 3-year target, recognizing the need to address the Technical, People Development, and Management issues that are related to OEE losses (covered in Chapter 4).

When using the OEE Loss Analysis, there are a number of structured steps, with the most important being the agreed assumptions behind each loss for best practice. For example, at one of our longest-serving clients, they have been conducting an OEE Loss Analysis on their bottling line each year for the past 10 years, resulting in more than doubling their output. In 2008, they used the following assumptions for Planned Downtime and Setup or Changeover Downtime:

Loss	Assumption	Ideal Vision
Planned Downtime	Allowed 2 hours per week per shift (2 shifts) for Operator Equipment Management (Autonomous Maintenance) activities during which Maintenance should be able to carry out most of their PMs, etc.; however, the remainder of maintenance will be carried out over No Production Required Time (most weekends). Line is also run continuously (no meal break downtime allowed for owing to allocated relief Operators to cover for the breaks)	5%
Setup Downtime	10 product changeovers per week with an allowance of 12 minutes per changeover = 2 hours per week	2.5%

The steps of conducting an OEE Loss Analysis are covered in detail in Chapter 5.

Once the assumptions are agreed upon, based on business requirements for each loss, then the gap between current performance "as-is" and future performance "ideal vision" can be identified.

> ***It is the ability to close the gap within an agreed timeframe that can be monitored and compared if necessary.***

We suggest that the gap be closed within 3 years, with approximately 50% achieved within the first 12 months. It is "how good this is being achieved" that can be compared or benchmarked between sites irrespective of what the actual OEE figure is.

TECHNICAL VERSUS PEOPLE DEVELOPMENT— RELATED OEE LOSSES

Example: a spring breaks on a machine resulting in a product being produced out of specification. Ideally, the machine would stop immediately after the spring breaks and the product goes out of specification. In this case, we have a Technical problem (spring worn out or spring inappropriate for the work required) and can be addressed by the maintenance people or a small Cross-functional Team of, say, machine designer, production person regarding operation parameters, maintenance person regarding servicing, and so on.

However, we may have a different scenario:

When the spring breaks, the machine does not stop automatically (could be an old machine that has not had quality problem sensing installed) and you start producing off specification output. During a quality check, the off-spec output is identified and the search starts for the cause of the problem—it may take a while for the offending broken spring to be identified. This is an example of People Development losses—the time to identify the problem and its causes. The aim of the 7 Steps of Operator Equipment Management or Autonomous Maintenance is to have Operators who understand the functioning of their equipment (role of the spring) and have an understanding of what conditions within their equipment could lead to quality problems (broken spring will result in a certain type of off-spec output). Unless the Technical solution of auto stopping when the spring breaks can be quickly and cheaply implemented, then the People Development loss will need to be addressed through Production Area Based Team improvement activities of Operator Equipment Management or Autonomous Maintenance.

When improving OEE, it is important to recognize that the losses need to be addressed from both ends of the Pareto chart and hence why it is important to take both a Technical issues focus and a People Development issues focus as outlined in Figure 1.6.

The Challenge of Productivity and OEE

OEE often does not take into account any changes in manning levels on a production line unless they are linked to the ideal speed; for example, with four people, we can produce **X per hour**, whereas with five people, we can produce **X + Y per hour**. Hence, depending on the manning levels, the Ideal Speed would change for calculating OEE.

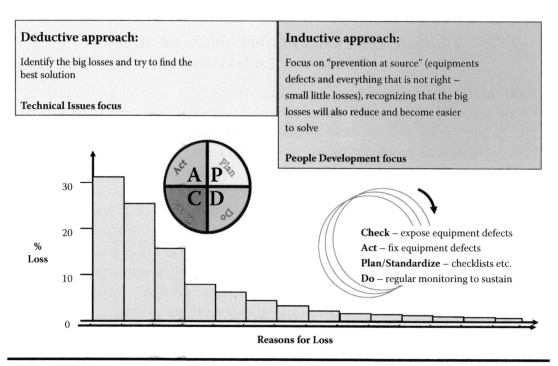

Figure 1.6   OEE improvement is about addressing losses from both ends of the Pareto chart rather than just focusing on the big losses.

We have seen many situations when OEE has been poor as a result of equipment or material problems, so extra people (often casuals) have been brought in to assist; however, there is no indication of this on the OEE performance charts.

Hence, OEE should be linked to an agreed direct labor level or Productivity (output per person hour) should be monitored in parallel with OEE performance—a practice rarely seen at sites or in benchmark studies.

Key Learnings from Chapter 1

- OEE is a powerful improvement tool if used correctly.
- Too often, misguided managers go looking for the simple measure that they can focus on to compare performance; however, in reality, there is no one measure that tells the full story.
- A suite of performance measures that are aligned to your site's Key Success Factors of Operations are required to capture all opportunities for improvement in an operation.
- To support the improvement of your suite of performance measures, we have found that OEE (plant and equipment focused) and Lead Time Reduction (process focused) are the drivers to improve, not measures to be compared.
- Production must be accountable for OEE performance with all other departments assisting them to achieve agreed targets of closing the gap.

Chapter 2

Measuring OEE

The Need for Standard Definitions

Many years back, we were working with an Australasian company that manufactured metal and plastic containers. At the time, they had about 14 sites throughout Australia and New Zealand. The National Operations Manager wanted to introduce Overall Equipment Effectiveness (OEE) measurement to all the sites so he could monitor equipment performance, so he copied various pages on OEE from the book *TPM Development Program* by Seiichi Nakajima, and asked all the plant engineers to calculate the OEE for a specific machine that was at all the sites. The interesting thing was that when we got them all together to discuss TPM and asked them each to share their OEE findings, the results ranged from 40% to 105%.

When we facilitated an open discussion on how they calculated their OEE performance, we found the following:

- Some had included planned downtime and some hadn't.
- Some had included setup time and some had concluded that setup times were planned downtime because they were dictated by the production schedule and there was a standard time allocated for them and hence unless they went over the time, it was planned downtime and hence didn't include it.
- Some had used a standard rate from production planning as their speed while others had actually identified an ideal speed for the machine, which was about 20% higher than the production planning speed.

The learning from the discussion was that the reason for the variation in OEE for the machines, which were all basically running at the same performance level, was lack of clearly defined standard definitions.

The Need to Determine the Operational Situation

The way you measure OEE can vary based on the Operational Situation. We have found that there are three main Operational Situations that may exist in a Manufacturing Plant. In some situations, you may find more than one occurring. The table below outlines the three main Operational Situations.

	Operational Situations		
	Fixed Time *Ongoing Schedule* *(e.g., Continuous* *Operation Plant)*	*Fixed Input* *Batch-Driven Schedule* *(e.g., Pharmaceutical,* *Adhesives, Pie Making)*	*Fixed Output* *Output-Driven Schedule* *(e.g., Bakery [Daily* *Fresh], Newspapers)*
Available time	**Fixed**	Variable	Variable
Inputs	Variable	**Fixed**	Variable
Good output	Variable	Variable	**Fixed**

The most common and simplest to manage is the **Fixed Time** situation, where the line is required to run whenever it is crewed. In **Fixed Input** situations, you may have occasions when the required "fixed" input has been processed and there is still crewed time available (e.g., they finished the batch an hour before the shift ends and there is no next batch prepared). **Fixed Output** situation can also result in a similar occasion when what is required to be made is completed before the end of the shift.

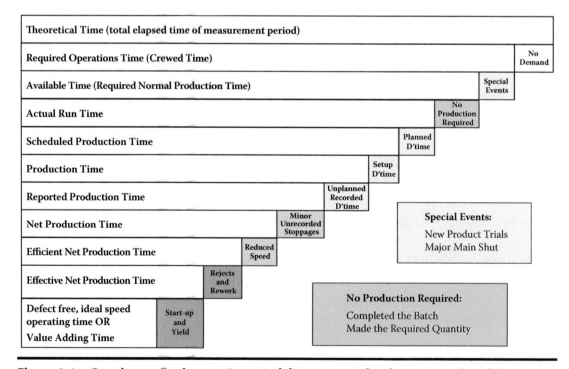

Figure 2.1   Creating an Equipment Loss Model to support the three Operational Situations.

An Equipment Loss Model that can accommodate the three Operational Situations is shown in Figure 2.1.

In the ***Fixed Time*** operational situation, **No Production Required** during Crewed Time will be Zero and hence **Available Time** and **Actual Run Time** would be the same.

As such, the **Actual Run Time** and **No Production Required** line can be deleted from the Loss Model.

In the ***Fixed Input*** and ***Fixed Output*** operational situations where **No Production Required** during Crewed Time may occur, this should be measured and monitored separately on a daily run chart, and reported (to the daily review meeting) along with OEE.

Equipment Performance Definitions

OEE is often not the only measure created when monitoring equipment performance as highlighted in Figure 2.2.

Line Utilization (LU)

This is an important measure at the corporate level to help determine when to buy new assets as opposed to running more shifts. It is also influenced by the marketing team's ability to sell the capacity of the Line, rather than a measure that the Operations Manager can significantly influence.

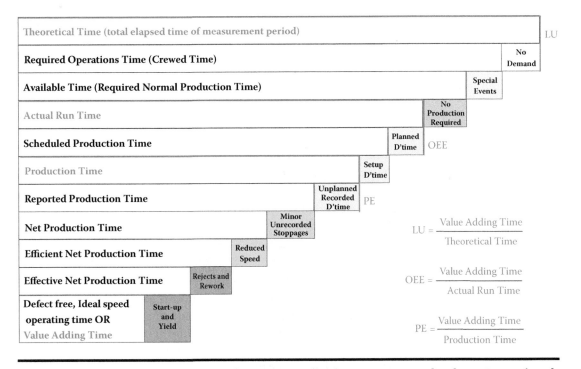

Figure 2.2 Creating Equipment Performance Definitions to support the three Operational Situations.

Overall Equipment Effectiveness (OEE)

This is an important measure at the site level to monitor line performance and can be used as an Improvement Driver that is correlated to the ability to make Good Output. It should never be used as a comparative measure.

Production Efficiency (PE)

This measure is often created to compare operating performance between lines as it removes Planned Downtime and Setup Downtime Losses, which can be unique to a particular line or site. Unfortunately, because it does not include Planned Downtime and Setup Downtime Losses, it can give a false sense of achievement as there can be significant improvement opportunities hidden.

Example Definitions Related to Equipment Losses

Once your Equipment Loss Model has been finalized, you need to develop a definition for each of the losses:

No Demand:	Planned and approved no run time authorized by production planners and management *at least 1 week in advance* owing to lack of customer orders and hence the line or equipment is not crewed.
Special Events:	Production time allocated for new product trials or major Maintenance time as in annual shutdown.
No Production Required:	Crewed Time when production is not required because the Batch has been completed or the required Good Output is achieved.
Planned Downtime:	Budgeted and approved downtime during Required Production Time authorized by management *at least 48 hours in advance*, for example, planned meal breaks if lines do not run continuously; planned maintenance periods; planned training or meetings requiring the line to stop; planned improvement time (CI Production Activities such as Work Area Management/5S or Operator Equipment Management/Autonomous Maintenance). *Note: Any extensions to the planned/authorized time to be classified as Unplanned Downtime.*
Setup or Changeover Downtime:	The elapsed time from last good output produced to the new good output produced at required speed following a setup or changeover to a different product. *Note: Some plants or equipment only run a dedicated product where this loss is zero and hence can be deleted from the Loss Model.*
Unplanned Recorded Downtime:	All downtime recorded (on the monitoring system or production records) other than Planned Downtime and Setup Downtime. This could include such losses as breakdowns or no feed. *Note: Some plants specify that only downtime greater than 10 (or 5) minutes must be recorded with the smaller losses being picked up as Minor Unrecorded Stoppages.*

Minor Unrecorded Stoppages:	All observed or calculated stoppages that have not been recorded. *Note: Details of these losses are normally identified by formal Cross-functional Improvement Teams during, say, 4–6 hours observation of the plant/equipment.*
Reduced Speed:	An allowance to compensate for slower than Ideal Speed over the whole of the Net Production Time.
Rejects and Rework:	An allowance to compensate for time lost based on the Ideal Speed for all output not right first time.
Start-up and Yield:	An allowance to compensate for time lost based on the Ideal Speed for all start-up and yield losses.

Next, you should define how you are going to determine Ideal Speed. We have identified three possible best practice ways of determining the Ideal Speed depending on the situation:

1. **Original Equipment Manufacturer's *Design Constraint* Speed**, which we define as the maximum speed that the critical piece of equipment could run at because of the limitations of its design. (This is quite different from Manufacturer's recommended speed, which is often slower.)
2. **Sampled Speed** of the critical piece of equipment **measured over a short period (e.g., 5 minutes)**, achievable with best operator, best feed, best environmental conditions, and best equipment conditions without "red lining" the equipment.
3. **Upper Control Limit Speed** of the daily or weekly run chart of the actual equipment speed of the critical piece of equipment over at least 15 points with any special causes removed.

On an integrated production line, the Ideal Speed should be determined for the critical piece of equipment that may or may not be the current bottleneck (e.g., on a filling line, it would be the filler); recognizing OEE will exclude any yield loss before the Ideal Speed measurement point, which, if an issue, will require a separate measure to identify and monitor.

It is worth noting that we often find different "speeds" being used in the workplace for specific purposes. The key is to recognize that they exist and ensure that there is no confusion regarding what speed you are referring to:

1. Standard Speed (used for Production Planning and Costing and is typically about 10%–20% lower than the Ideal Speed)
2. Optimum Speed (the maximum you will allow line to be run as a result of current conditions so as to minimize quality issues)
3. Ideal Speed (used for calculating OEE as per definitions noted above)
4. Typical Speed (based on current practices)
5. Required Speed (based on supply constraints or customer demand—used to measure Required Equipment Effectiveness)

As such, it is important that people do not confuse Ideal Speed (designed to assist improvement) with speed or rate used for costing or scheduling.

Key Learnings from Chapter 2

- Create your Loss Model and document your definitions so that there is agreement by all, recognizing that "measures dictate behavior."
- Different operational situations may need a different approach to measuring OEE.

Chapter 3

Calculating OEE

As mentioned in Chapter 1, Overall Equipment Effectiveness (OEE) can be calculated either by using Equations or by using the Time or Unit Loss Model. We have found calculating OEE using the Time Loss Model to be most helpful when capturing a detailed analysis of all the losses.

We have also found that, at many sites, current continuous recording of losses may not be that accurate when it comes to minor stops or reasons for downtime. As such, we suggest using several observations of about 4–5 hours duration to identify any shortfalls in continuous recording data. Below are the results of an observation conducted by four team members over 4 hours with each spending an hour observing a 4-L Paint Can manufacturing line.

Event/Loss	Time
Theoretical time—time of observation (4 Paint Can)	240 minute(s)
No demand	0 minute(s)
New product trial time (special event)	40 minute(s)
Planned downtime (morning tea)	10 minute(s)
Setup downtime (1 off)	16 minute(s)
Unplanned recorded downtime (2 off)	24 minute(s) (total)
Minor unrecorded stoppages (30 off)	40 minute(s) (total)
Total amount processed	1020 units
Total rejects and rework	20 units
Start-up and yield loss	0 units
Good output produced	1000 units
Actual production speed[a]	9.27 units/minute(s)
Ideal speed	10 units/minute(s)

[a] Identified by a short period measurement during the observation.

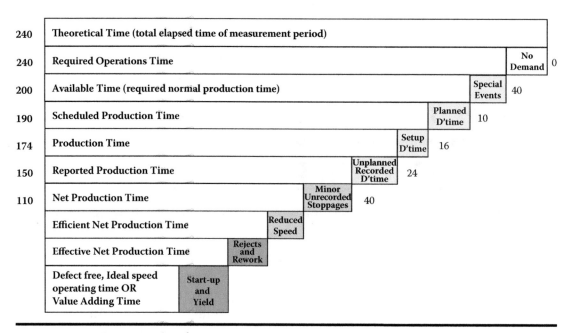

240	Theoretical Time (total elapsed time of measurement period)							
240	Required Operations Time						No Demand	0
200	Available Time (required normal production time)					Special Events	40	
190	Scheduled Production Time				Planned D'time	10		
174	Production Time			Setup D'time	16			
150	Reported Production Time		Unplanned Recorded D'time	24				
110	Net Production Time	Minor Unrecorded Stoppages	40					
	Efficient Net Production Time	Reduced Speed						
	Effective Net Production Time	Rejects and Rework						
	Defect free, Ideal speed operating time OR Value Adding Time	Start-up and Yield						

Figure 3.1   Calculating OEE in a Fixed Time operational situation using the Time Loss Model with observation recorded data inserted.

The above data was then inserted into a Time Loss model, as shown in Figure 3.1. The remaining three losses of Reduced Speed, Rejects & Rework, and Start-up & Yield need to be calculated using the equations in Figure 3.2.

These figures can now be put back into the Time Loss Model (Figure 3.3).

We are now in a position to calculate OEE using the Time Loss equation:

Reduced Speed Losses (time):

$$\frac{\text{Net Production Time (minute)} \times [\text{Ideal Speed (units/minute)} - \text{Actual Speed (units/minute)}]}{\text{Ideal Speed (units/minute)}}$$

$$\frac{110 \times [10 - 9.27]}{10} = 8 \text{ minutes*}$$

$$\frac{110 \times 0.73}{10} = 8.03*$$

*Round to closest minute

Rejects and Rework Losses (time):

$$\frac{\text{Total Rejects and Rework (units)}}{\text{Ideal Speed (units/minute)}}$$

$$\frac{20}{10} = 2 \text{ minutes}$$

Start-up and Yield Losses (time):

$$\frac{\text{Total Start-up and Yield Loss (units)}}{\text{Ideal Speed (units/minute)}}$$

$$\frac{0}{10} = 0 \text{ minute}$$

Figure 3.2   Equations to assist calculating OEE using the Time Loss approach.

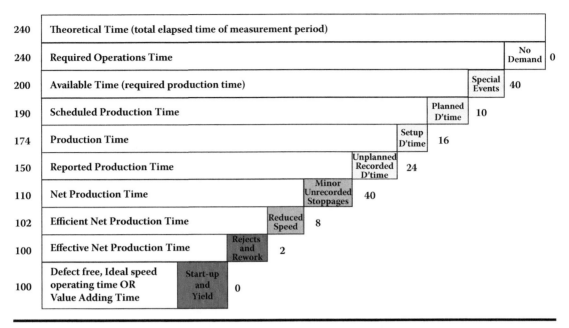

240	Theoretical Time (total elapsed time of measurement period)										
240	Required Operations Time									No Demand	0
200	Available Time (required production time)								Special Events	40	
190	Scheduled Production Time							Planned D'time	10		
174	Production Time						Setup D'time	16			
150	Reported Production Time					Unplanned Recorded D'time	24				
110	Net Production Time				Minor Unrecorded Stoppages	40					
102	Efficient Net Production Time			Reduced Speed	8						
100	Effective Net Production Time		Rejects and Rework	2							
100	Defect free, Ideal speed operating time OR Value Adding Time	Start-up and Yield	0								

Figure 3.3   Calculating OEE in a Fixed Time operational situation using the Time Loss Model with observation calculated data inserted.

$$\text{OEE} = \text{Value Adding Time/Available Time}$$

which, from the Time Loss model developed, is: 100/200 = 50%.

To verify our answer, we can use the High-Level OEE (HLOEE) equation we developed earlier in Chapter 1:

$$\text{HLOEE} = \text{Good Output Produced/(Available Time} \times \text{Ideal Speed)}$$

which, from the data collected during the observation, is: 1000/(200 × 10) = 50%.

As mentioned earlier, the HLOEE equation is a much simpler and quicker way of calculating OEE; however, it does not provide the details of where all the losses are coming from as outlined in the Time Loss Model approach.

Using the Loss Information

The reason for collecting Loss information is to make improvement decisions. One of the most commonly used tools for this is the Pareto chart.

To create a Pareto chart of the data collected in our Time Loss Model, we need to move the minutes into a percentage, as shown in Figure 3.4.

The First-Level Pareto chart can now be created as shown in Figure 3.5.

From the First-Level Pareto, we notice that the Minor Unrecorded Stoppages are the greatest loss at 20%. Obviously, we would look at all the losses; however, the benefit of the Pareto Analysis is that it highlights the largest Loss and hopefully the one with the biggest potential for improvement.

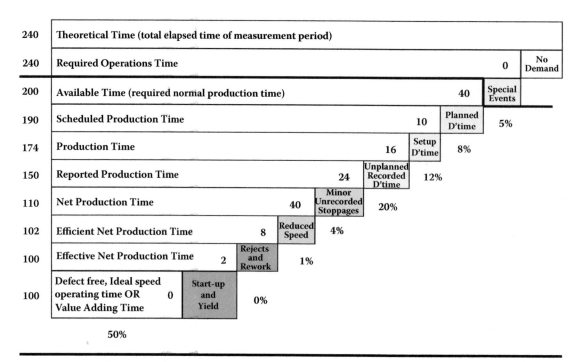

Figure 3.4   Calculating OEE in a Fixed Time operational situation using the Time Loss Model with observation loss percentages inserted.

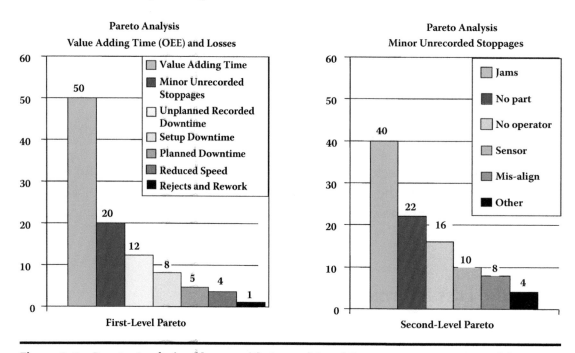

Figure 3.5   Pareto Analysis of losses with Second-Level Pareto as a percentage of the 20% loss which totals 100%.

To demonstrate this, a Second-Level Pareto chart has been created for the Minor Unrecorded Stoppages based on the information collected during the observation. In many cases after the first observation, a second and maybe third observation would be conducted with a greater focus on collecting the required data to allow creating meaningful Second-Level Pareto charts.

The other thing we find helpful is to express the Second-Level Pareto Analysis in terms of percentage of the Loss being measured (Figure 3.6).

By viewing the Second-Level Pareto chart, we see that Jams contributes to 8 percentage points of OEE loss and becomes the obvious candidate for further analysis to identify possible corrective actions to eliminate or minimize the loss.

As mentioned, this example was taken from a 4-L Paint Can manufacturing line as shown in Photo 3.1. The line was set up in a U shape, with the body of the can being rolled and seam welded on the left before being rolled down a long chute to the machine that attached the base and top to the can body. It then moved to the right to have the handle attached.

In Photo 3.1, you can see the tight S section of the chute before it feeds into the machine (the shiny can bodies can be seen on the feed chute directly on the left of the central machine).

On investigation, the team found that on occasions, the can bodies would get caught up in the tight S-shaped section of the chute and the central machine would run out of feed and stop. This required the Operator to pick up a bar and bang the side of the chute until the can bodies started rolling again (if you look closely, marks can be seen on the side of the S-shaped chute). This accounted for 40% of the Minor Unrecorded Stoppages that were picked up by the team during their observations and which equated to 8 percentage points of OEE loss as outlined in the Second-Level Pareto Analysis.

The team asked the Operators how long the problem had been there and had they told anyone about it. They couldn't remember exactly when it started; however, they thought it was about 9 months ago just after they introduced a new can body design. Shortly after it started to be a problem, they mentioned it to the Maintenance

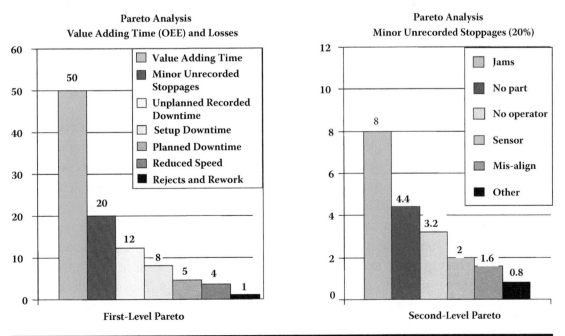

Figure 3.6 Pareto Analysis of losses with Second-Level Pareto as a percentage of the OEE loss which totals 20%.

Photo 3.1   4-liter Paint Can manufacturing line.

department and they arranged for a bigger and stronger bar for them so they didn't have to stretch and hit the chute as many times to free up the can bodies! They also said that about 3 months ago when they introduced 5S, someone came along and installed some hooks for them to hang the bar on, so it was always there when they needed it rather than sometimes having to waste time searching for it!

The team did further investigations and found that the new can body intro-duced some 9 months back did have a tendency to jam in the S-shaped section of the chute if it got slightly out of alignment as it rolled down. With this knowledge, the maintenance people found a spare S-shaped section of chute and modified it to eliminate the problem. They then replaced the chute during a lunch break, and within 2 weeks, the new chute was in and the jamming problem eliminated. This gave them an 8-percentage point gain in OEE taking it from 50% to 58%.

The team then revisited the Second-Level Pareto chart of Minor Unrecorded Stoppages and, recognizing they had little control over No Part or No Operator, identified that the Sensor issue of 2 percentage points could be worth investigat-ing. What they discovered was that one of the gearbox output shafts was leaking oil that was splattering onto a sensor in the machine that indicated if there were no bases ready for attachment to the body. As such, as the oil built up on the sensor, the sensor would intermittently fail and the machine would stop. To get around the problem, the Operator used a compressed air line to blast air at the sensor and hopefully clear it enough to get going. Unfortunately, this significantly reduced the life of the sensor, resulting in its regular replacement by Maintenance. After fur-ther investigation, it was realized that to properly fix the oil leak problem, it would require significant downtime on the machine, and this was best done during the next Christmas maintenance period, which was only a couple of months away.

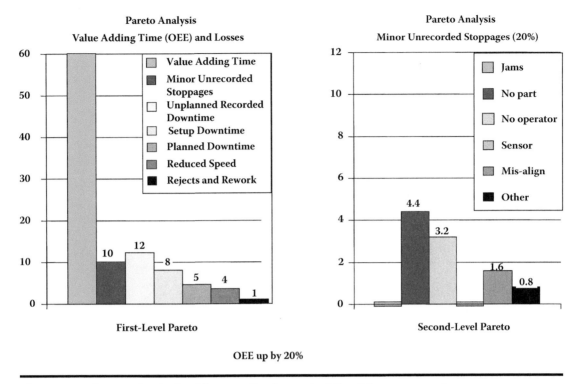

Figure 3.7 Pareto Analysis of losses after impact of the 2 improvements.

In the meantime, they asked the Operators if they trained them and gave them a special rag, could they wipe the sensor each morning before starting the machine to ensure there would be no build-up of oil and no need to use the compressed air. They explained that this would only be required until the Christmas shutdown when maintenance would fix the problem. The Operators were quite happy to do this minor task as the team had helped them by eliminating the need to bang the chute with a bar. As such, the Sensor loss of 2 percentage points was eliminated and the OEE moved from 58% to 60% (Figure 3.7).

The total impact of the two improvements was to move OEE from 50% to 60%, which resulted in a 20% improvement in the capacity of the machine each shift. The other benefits were that you had Operators who were less frustrated with the machine and a Maintenance person less frustrated because they didn't have to replace the sensor all the time.

Key Learnings from Chapter 3

- There are two ways of calculating OEE, by Equations and by using Time Loss, with both giving the same OEE result but with different detail.
- High Level OEE or HLOEE is a very simple and accurate way to calculate OEE; however, it does not outline where the losses are coming from.
- Pareto Analysis of losses is a helpful tool, if used correctly, to identify OEE improvements.

Chapter 4

Improving OEE

What Affects the OEE Losses?

Before trying to improve Overall Equipment Effectiveness (OEE) losses, we need to have a broad understanding of what issues affect the 7 Losses (Figure 4.1).

We have found that there are three types of issues that can affect OEE losses:

1. **Technical** issues
2. **People Development** issues
3. **Management** issues

As such, as we analyze OEE, we need to highlight or classify the losses into these issues so that we address them appropriately.

Our learning has been that Technical issues tend to be best addressed by Cross-functional Team improvement activities and People Development issues are best addressed by Production Area Based Team improvement activities such as Work Area Management/5S and the 7 Steps of Operator Equipment Management/Autonomous Maintenance.

The Management issues are associated with Planned Downtime and cover how much time should be allocated or allowed for specific activities; however, sometimes, they are linked to Agreements or Contracts with the workforce and may take time to negotiate changes such as whether you stop the line for breaks or have relief personnel and keep the line running.

Some of the typical planned downtime losses affected by management decisions are as follows:

- Planned Maintenance—do we undertake it during nonproduction time such as weekends or production rostered days off, or do we not do planned maintenance and just run to failure, or do we incorporate it into Production Area Based Team Clean for Inspection improvement time.

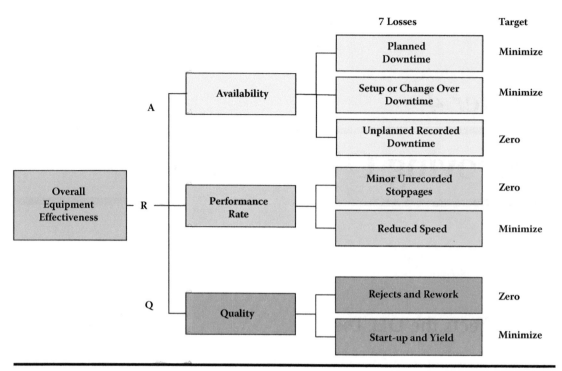

Figure 4.1   OEE Model.

- Team Daily Review/Toolbox Meeting—how long and when.
- Planned Start of Shift Downtime—do we require start-up prechecks.
- Paid Breaks Downtime—do we have relief people and not stop the line or do we all stop for the breaks.
- Planned End of Shift Downtime—do we require shutdown checks or cleans.
- Production Area Based Team Improvement Time (Work Area Management/5S and 7 Steps of Operator Equipment Management/ Autonomous Maintenance activity)—how much time should be allocated each week and when.
- Other Planned Downtime—do we have regular communication or safety briefings.

Capturing OEE Loss Analysis Data

There are three ways of capturing OEE Loss Analysis data:

1. ***High-Level Measurement***

    This is the most accurate measure of OEE; however, it does not highlight where the losses are coming from, but it does highlight how much Loss you must identify.

2. ***Continuous Recording***

    The accuracy of data can be quite low, especially the reason for the loss, when a lot of losses are occurring (i.e., when OEE is below 60%); however, by working with the Operators for a set period of time (e.g., over the next 2 or 3 weeks) and by explaining the need, simplifying the capture method, and providing regular feedback, more meaningful data should be able to be obtained.

3. *Sampling through Observations*

This will not give a true representation of all the losses attributed to the duration and frequency of the sample; however, it should identify the Minor Unrecorded Losses and the Unplanned Interventions.

Conducting an OEE Loss Analysis

The steps of conducting an OEE Loss Analysis can be broken up into the following:

1. Establish previous 6 weeks OEE Baseline (or other relevant time frame that captures the majority or greater than 90% of the products) using High-Level OEE equation.
2. Conduct a detailed OEE Loss Analysis, engaging all people in the area to determine "as-is" situation.
3. Document assumptions based on business requirements and best practice for each loss ("ideal vision" in, say, 3 years once the 7 Steps of Operator Equipment Management or Autonomous Maintenance covering Clean for Inspections, Train for Inspections, and Manage by Inspections have been successfully completed).
4. Develop "12-month Vision" targets.
5. Identify and verify the causes of each loss (other than Planned Downtime) and classify them into Technical or People Development opportunities.
6. Determine the cost impact of each loss based on agreed upon assumptions.
7. Develop an improvement action plan for the next 12 months and link it to the 5-year Continuous Improvement Master Plan.

Getting Started

Once the initial pilot production areas or lines where OEE can be measured have been selected by your Continuous Improvement or CI Leadership Team, we recommend a Cross-functional Team of six to eight people that meet for up to 1.5 hours each week over 12 weeks (so as not to disrupt their normal duties) be established in each area with the mandate to conduct a diagnostic on current performance including the following:

■ Identify all equipment and process losses and wastes (including all unplanned interventions or occasions when Operators need to touch the equipment even though it does not stop) for the production area or line while engaging all people working in the area to contribute their ideas on opportunities for improvement.

■ Create a 3-year Ideal Vision of performance based on documented assumptions so as to determine the gap between Current Performance and Ideal Performance.

■ Implement any small "immediate action" improvements approved by the manager on the team.

■ Determine possible root cause solutions to sufficient losses so as to improve OEE by at least 10%–25% while also improving or maintaining the Goal Aligned Performance Measures in the area (e.g., safety, quality, delivery, etc).

■ At week 6, present the outcomes from the diagnostic analysis and proposed action plan to achieve the target OEE improvement for the CI Leadership Team to approve.

■ Implement the agreed improvements and capture all learning.

■ Identify further improvement initiatives involving Cross-functional Teams (to address Technical issues) and Production Area Based Teams progressing Work Area Management/5S and Operator Equipment Management/ Autonomous Maintenance (to address People Development issues) so as to achieve the 3-year Ideal Vision identified above.

■ At week 12, present the outcomes and learning, along with recommendations to achieve the Ideal Vision of OEE performance to the CI Leadership Team.

We refer to this type of team as a Macro Focused Equipment & Process Improvement Team as it is taking a "big picture or macro" look at all the losses across the entire production area or line. Later on, when specific losses have been identified, the site might create Micro Focused Equipment & Process Teams to address all the losses in a particular section of the Production Area or Line, or they may create a Special Micro Focused Equipment & Process Improvement Team to address a specific loss across the production area or line.

The typical makeup of a Macro Focused Equipment & Process Improvement Team would be

Macro Focused Equipment & Process Improvement Team (6–8 members) **Focus: Defined Production Area**	
1	Level 1 Salary Person responsible for the Area—lead the Team
1	Frontline Leader for Area (wages) or Senior Operator
1	Operator
1–2	Maintainers responsible for Area (Mechanical & Electrical)
1–2	Tech Support responsible for Area (provide horsepower for analysis)
1	Leadership Team Member (Manager)
Plus each team would be facilitated by CI Coordinator (internal resource) CI Specialist or Navigator (external resource if required)	

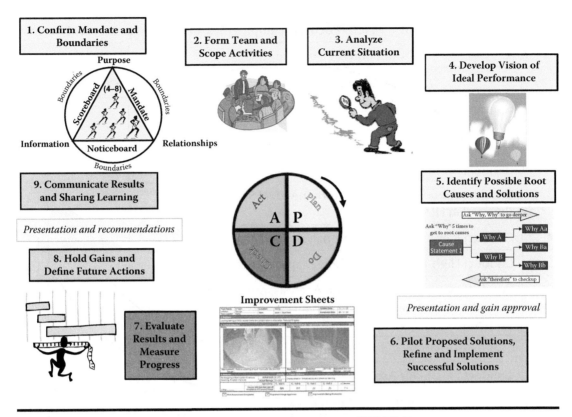

Figure 4.2   Focused Equipment & Process Improvement (FE&PI) Process.

In selecting the team members, it is important that they are all on the same rotating shift or on dayshift so that all meetings can be held during normal work time.

We recommend that Focused Equipment & Process Improvement Teams follow a proven nine-step process supported by a prescriptive Team Member Manual to assist them to achieve their mandate (Figure 4.2). Typically, the teams will commence with a 4 hour kick-off workshop and then each team will meet for up to 1.5 hours a week for the next 12 weeks. After their week 12 presentation, the team would be congratulated and then disbanded, with team members being allocated to further Cross-functional Improvement Teams.

Preparation before Kicking-Off Teams

To assist each team to get a head start on their analysis, we have found the following checklist and support information very useful for your CI Coordinator/ Manager to work through with the support of the CI Leadership Team so that the information can be presented to the team at their kick-off workshop.

During the kick-off workshop, the team should be given the opportunity to challenge or enhance the analysis (if required) so as to gain ownership to it.

This way, there is less time commitment by the team members before moving into the interesting part, that is, doing activities such as Operator Surveys, Operator Knowledge Base Analysis, Maintenance Knowledge Base Analysis, and the OEE Loss Analysis including Observations.

Preparation Checklist for a Macro Focused Equipment & Process Improvement Team

	Production Area or Line		Kick-Off Date	
No.	*Description of Task Required*	*Who*	*Comments*	☑
1	Conduct Future Analysis to ensure team can proceed with certainty			☐
2	Conduct Product/Output Analysis to determine boundaries of HLOEE calculation for team			☐
3	Conduct Speed Analysis to determine Ideal Speed(s) to be used in HLOEE calculation			☐
4	Conduct Raw Materials/Input Analysis			☐
5	Conduct High-Level Process Flow Map Analysis			☐
6	Conduct Information Collection Analysis, prepare recommendations for team if enhancements are required			☐
7	Conduct Structure and Roster Analysis			☐
8	Conduct Base Skills Analysis			☐
9	Conduct Production Planning Analysis			☐
10	Conduct Baseline Analysis			☐
11	Confirm OEE and Loss definitions to be used by team			☐
12	Prepare OEE Loss Analysis Spreadsheet outlining the sections identified in the High-Level Process Map Analysis and appropriate Planned Downtime elements			☐
13	Collect weekly Good Output Produced, Available Time, and Ideal Speed for the past 6 weeks to allow the HLOEE exercise to be completed during the kick-off workshop (OEE Measurement training session) and assist with the OEE Baseline			☐
14	Establish means to collect "Processed Amount" so that the Quality mass balance equation can be used to calculate Quality Loss, which may also assist with the OEE Baseline			☐
15	Establish OEE Baseline based on the previous 6 weeks' performance excluding any special causes and populate the Baseline Analysis column on the Second-Level OEE Loss Analysis Sheet recognizing that there may be significant gaps regarding the details; however, the HLOEE should be accurate			☐
16	Prepare a Kick-off presentation, incorporating the results of all the analyses to date			☐

Preparation Analysis for a Macro Focused Equipment & Process Improvement Team

The objective of the preparation is to conduct initial background analysis for the production area or line to allow briefing of the team during their kick-off workshop so that there is more time for the team to get into the critical analysis items.

The 10 key tasks conducted during the preparation, which match the first 10 tasks of the preparation checklist, are as follows:

1. Future Analysis
2. Product/Output Analysis
3. Speed Analysis
4. Raw Materials/Input Analysis
5. High-Level Process Flow Map Analysis
6. Information Collection Analysis
7. Structure and Roster Analysis
8. Base Skills Analysis
9. Production Planning Analysis
10. Defined Area Baseline Analysis

1. Future Analysis—What changes do we expect in the near future?

Purpose: To provide the team with an understanding of any expected changes, which may affect team decisions and ensures all improvement actions are in line with future projects and changes.

For example, over the next 6 months:

■ Changes to current
   – Production Demand
   – Product Mix
   – Raw Materials
   – Technology
   – Resources
■ Addition or Removal of Plant and Equipment.
■ Addition or Deletion of other improvement initiatives that will consume or release resources.

2. Product/Output Analysis

Purpose: To understand the range of products/outputs associated with the line and whether there is a quality standard for each and, from an analysis perspective, whether they can be grouped into similar families.

Obtain a copy of all SKUs (unique outputs) and check off if there is a clear visual quality standard that is used to verify compliance.

Where appropriate, group SKUs into Product Families, which have similar process and run speeds (e.g., 1-L range of flavors or colors, 0.5-L range of flavors or colors, etc.).

3. Speed Analysis

Purpose: To understand the various speeds associated with the line and what the ideal speed or speeds should be for calculating OEE.

Using the data collected from the Product/Output Analysis, list the following:

1. Standard Speed (used for Production Planning and Costing)
2. Optimum Speed (the maximum you will allow line to be run owing to current conditions so as to minimize quality issues)
3. Ideal Speed (used for calculating OEE as per definition noted)
4. Typical Speed (based on current practices)
5. Required Speed (to match supply or customer demand) if appropriate

#	Product/Product Family	Standard Speed	Optimum Speed	Ideal Speed	Typical Speed	Required Speed
1						
2						

On an integrated production line, the Ideal Speed should be determined for the critical piece of equipment that may or may not be the current bottleneck (e.g., on a filling line, it would be the filler); recognizing OEE will exclude any yield loss before the Ideal Speed measurement point, which, if an issue, will require a separate measure to identify and monitor.

4. Raw Materials/Input Analysis

Purpose: To understand the impact of variability in raw materials/inputs on OEE performance.

1. Does variability in Raw Materials cause variability in line performance?
2. If this is an issue, what process or processes are (or should be) in place to monitor and minimize this?
3. Does variability in other Inputs (e.g., labeling, packaging, release agents, energy, etc.) cause variability in line performance?
4. If this is an issue, what process or processes are (or should be) in place to monitor and minimize this?

If necessary, list all raw materials or inputs including pack size (if appropriate) that cause problems/issues, noting whether a quality standard or spec exists, typical run time before replacement (e.g., roll of labels), and typical setup time (e.g., time to replace roll of labels).

Example Raw Materials/Inputs Sheet

#	Raw Material/ Inputs	Pack Size	Does Quality Standard/ Spec Exist?	Is Variability an Issue?	Typical Run Time	Typical Setup Time
1						
2						

5. High-Level Process Flow Map Analysis

Purpose: To create a High-Level Process Flow Map (Block Diagram) outlining all inputs and outputs for the production area or line to identify any possible variables that may affect performance (e.g., OEE) (Figure 4.3).

1. Where appropriate, note capability (output/time) for each block.
2. Identify where quality can be monitored/checks are conducted.
3. Identify where performance reporting occurs.
4. Identify where people are located and number (suggest use face icons with a different color for the Frontline Leader).
5. Divide the production area or line into sections for future analysis by Micro Focused Equipment & Process Improvement Teams (suggest at least four sections with the maximum being seven). These sections will be used in the Second-Level OEE Improvement Analysis sheet.

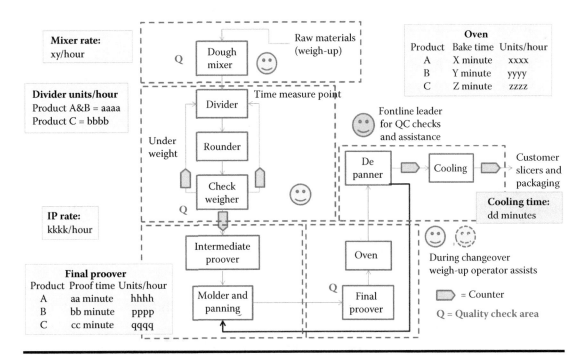

Figure 4.3   Example High-Level Process Flow Map Analysis.

6. Information Collection Analysis

Purpose: To identify what information is generated within the production area or line and assess whether appropriate and sufficient.

1. Collect a copy of all information generated during the following week.
2. If information is entered directly into a computer system, bring a copy of the relevant reports generated from this information.
3. Review the information to identify whether it is complete enough to allow completion of the Second-Level OEE Loss Analysis once the four to seven sections of the production area or line have been finalized. If not, determine the actions required.

7. Structure and Roster Analysis

Purpose: To understand the people impact on OEE performance and whether the structure and rosters will allow for the successful introduction of Production Area Based Team improvement activities such as Work Area Management/5S and the 7 Steps of Operator Equipment Management/Autonomous Maintenance.

1. Is there a competent production Frontline Leader each shift responsible for the performance of the crew and the production area or line?
2. How many people are required to operate the production area or line each shift (refer to the High-Level Process Map Analysis)?
3. Does the number of Operators assigned to the production area or line change, and if so, will this affect OEE?
4. Do the skills of Operators assigned to the production area or line change, and if so, will this affect OEE?
5. How many shifts are there and what time frame do they cover?
6. Are the shifts fixed or do they rotate (if they rotate what is the frequency)?
7. What is the policy to cover absenteeism?
8. What is the roster system of the Mechanical and Electrical Maintenance coverage and is it aligned or supportive?

8. Base Skills Analysis

Purpose: To determine whether the structure and Base Skills (ability to operate to agreed upon standard each workstation within the defined area) will allow for the successful introduction of Production Area Based Team improvement activities such as Work Area Management/5S and the 7 Steps of Operator Equipment Management/Autonomous Maintenance.

1. Is there a Base Skills Matrix established for each crew/shift?
2. Is the Base Skills Matrix up to date?
3. Is the Base Skills Matrix based on measurable Objective assessments?

Name	Workstation 1 Operate plus quality checks on inputs and outputs	Workstation 2 Operate plus quality checks on inputs and outputs	Workstation 3 Operate plus quality checks on inputs and outputs	Workstation 4 Operate plus quality checks on inputs and outputs	Workstation 5 Operate plus quality checks on inputs and outputs
Team Leader	4	4	4	4	4
Member 2	1	3	1	2	1
Member 3	1	2	3	1	2
Member 4	1	1	1	3	1
Member 5	2	1	3	1	3
Member 6	4	2	1	3	1

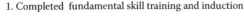

1. Completed fundamental skill training and induction

2. Can complete 8 process cycles in correct sequence with all safety and quality key points followed, no spillage, and with no quality outflows during the shift

3. Can complete 24 process cycles as above, with no quality outflows for 60 shifts

4. Completed job instructor training and successfully delivered training

Figure 4.4 Example of a Production Area Based Team Basic Base Skills Matrix.

4. Is there sufficient flexibility with each crew/shift to allow for future Area Based Team improvement activity such as Work Area Management/5S and the 7 Steps of Operator Equipment Management/Autonomous Maintenance?
5. Is there a need to improve the flexibility and stability of any of the crews/shifts?
6. Do we need to recommend an Education & Training Base Skills Team be established to address any of the above issues?

Note: If a proper Base Skills Matrix doesn't exist, normally there is no need to take on the task of creating one, as this is best addressed through establishing an Education & Training Operator Base Skills Team (Figure 4.4).

9. Production Planning Analysis

Purpose: To determine whether the current production planning process affects OEE Performance.

1. Obtain a copy of the planning rules for all Products or Product Families run through the production area or line to verify that they are accurate and current. Things covered should include typical run quantities, standard speed/run time, allowance for changeover/setup, allowance for CIP/Sanitization, allowance for over/under quantity, minimum batch quantity, product sequence rules, change of plan rules, frequency of issue rules, and so on.
2. Determine Stability of the Production Plan (changes per week/day and impact on OEE performance).

3. Determine the percentage of time allocated for Changeover/Setup Time each week.
4. Determine whether the current production planning process will impede future regular weekly Production Area Based Team improvement activities such as Work Area Management/5S and the 7 Steps of Operator Equipment Management/Autonomous Maintenance.

10. Production Area or Line Baseline Analysis

Purpose: To establish appropriate performance measures for the production area or line using the site Key Success Factors for Operations framework and then to establish a Baseline (stake-in-the-ground of current performance) and the Ideal Vision targets for each performance measure (Figure 4.5).

Ensure that the Cause and Effect performance measures that the team could have an impact on are covered in the Baseline (including costs such as scrap, maintenance, energy, etc). If these measures don't currently exist for the production area or line, they should be immediately established.

Where possible, weekly run charts should be established on the team's Scoreboard so that the impact of improvements can be monitored.

Note: These measures should also be used for Daily Management/Reactive Improvement for the production area or line and, when appropriate, Area Based Team daily review meetings.

The report back to the team during the kick-off workshop would include an explanation of the Key Success Factors and the allocated performance measures under each Key Success Factor.

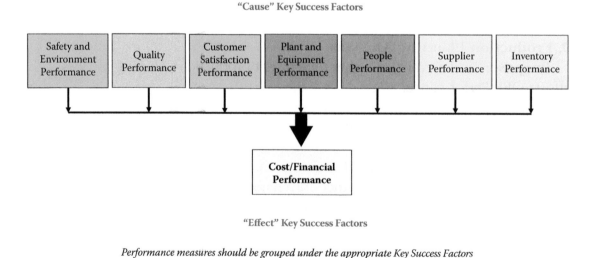

Figure 4.5 Example Key Success Factors for Operations.

OEE Loss Analysis Spreadsheet

To assist teams to conduct the OEE Loss Analysis, we have created an OEE Loss Analysis template consisting of a series of eight linked spreadsheets to help teams take a more structured and logical approach.

To conduct your own OEE Loss Analysis, obtain the Microsoft Excel file containing the eight linked spreadsheets of the OEE Loss Analysis spreadsheet by emailing CTPM on ctpm@ctpm.org.au.

Develop Your Planned Downtime Model for the Production Area or Line

Planned Downtime is an important part of the OEE Loss Model and should be broken down into its proper categories for later analysis. Typical Planned Downtime events may include the following:

■ Planned Maintenance
■ Team Daily Review/Toolbox Meeting
■ Planned Start of Shift Downtime
■ Paid Breaks Downtime
■ Planned End of Shift Downtime
■ Production Area Based Team Improvement Time—Work Area Management/5S and 7 Steps of Operator Equipment Management/ Autonomous Maintenance activity
■ Other Planned Downtime

Once identified and agreed upon, each category should be entered into the Second-Level OEE Loss Analysis Sheet.

Establish Your OEE Baseline

This should be completed by the CI Coordinator before the team is kicked-off and the cycle is commenced.

It typically involves reviewing the production records for the previous 6 weeks (or other relevant time frame to capture the majority or at least 90% of the products) and trying to gather as much loss information as possible. The critical thing is to identify what the Good Output was each week, how long the line or machine was scheduled to run for each week, and what the Ideal Speed of the line or machine has been defined as. With this information, the High-Level OEE can be calculated for each week with the average (excluding any agreed upon special causes that distort the average) for the 6 weeks being the Baseline for the production area or line.

If more detailed information about certain losses is available, it should also be captured and be available for the team to enter in the Baseline Analysis column of the Second-Level OEE Loss Analysis Sheet.

Provide OEE Training for Team Members

It is very important that those chosen to form the Cross-functional Team to conduct an OEE Loss Analysis have a good understanding of OEE. This can be done over a series of training events, or as one training event, or incorporated into the team kick-off workshop. We have found that any OEE training should involve the use of an appropriate hands-on simulation and working through relevant calculation and graphing exercises.

Below is an example of the content of a possible half-day OEE training session.

Section	Contents
1. Understanding OEE	1. Why was OEE developed? 2. Overall Equipment Effectiveness Model 3. What affects the OEE Losses? 4. Who should be Responsible and Accountable for OEE? 5. Calculating OEE using Time Loss and Equations 6. Calculating and Graphing High-Level OEE exercise 7. Identifying Best Practice OEE Targets 8. Understanding the Elements of OEE 9. Limitations of OEE as an Improvement Driver
2. Defining and Measuring OEE	10. The 3 Operational Situations (if relevant) 11. Creating an Equipment Loss Model 12. Creating Equipment Performance Definitions 13. Creating Equipment Loss Definitions and Why 14. Determining Ideal Speed and definition for site 15. Calculating OEE from an Observation exercise 16. Summary of OEE Measurement
3. Improving OEE	17. Improving OEE from an Observation
4. Practical Application	18. OEE Simulation
5. Monitoring OEE	19. Initial Capture of OEE Losses 20. Ongoing Reporting of OEE Performance

Team Kick-Off Workshop

The purpose of the Team kick-off workshop is to bond the team with a clear purpose and time frames, establish roles and rules, understand the importance of using facts and data for decision making rather than just experience and "gut feel," review the 10 pre-team analysis outlined previously, and allocate initial tasks toward completing step 3—Analyze Current Situation.

An effective kick-off workshop typically takes 4 hours and covers steps 1, 2, and part of step 3 as per the nine-step Focused Equipment & Process Improvement process outlined earlier in this chapter.

Key Learnings from Chapter 4

- There are three types of issues that can affect OEE Losses: Technical, People Development, and Management.
- There are three ways of capturing OEE Losses: High Level Measurement, Continuous Recording, and Sampling through Observation.
- An OEE Loss & Improvement Analysis is best done with a properly structured Cross-functional Team as the self-learning, especially from the observations, will challenge current beliefs and build relationships.
- Preparation Analysis properly conducted by the CI Coordinator/Manager and overseen by the CI Leadership Team is critical for the success of the Cross-functional Team.
- Developing your Planned Downtime Model and establishing the OEE Baseline should also be completed before kicking off the Cross-functional Team.

Chapter 5

Using the OEE Loss Analysis Spreadsheet

As mentioned in Chapter 4, to obtain the Microsoft Excel file containing the eight linked spreadsheets of the OEE Loss Analysis spreadsheet, e-mail CTPM on ctpm@ctpm.org.au.

To demonstrate the use of the OEE Loss Analysis Spreadsheet, we will use a bottling line example, which has an ideal speed of 1000 bottles per minute at the Filler and runs two 8-hour shift per day, 5 days/week. The data was collected over a 3-week period to ensure that the full range of product changes occurred and there were no major changes to the line or any special events. The line did not run any overtime for the 3-week period and there were no planned breaks so it ran for a total of 80 hours each week.

The analysis was conducted by a Macro Focused Equipment & Process Improvement cross-functional improvement team over a 13-week period or cycle where they started with a 4 hour kick-off workshop followed by twelve 1.5-hour meetings. The team reported progress on a weekly basis to the CI Leadership Team and also gave a formal midway 30-minute presentation to ensure their analysis was understood and agreed to by management, and approval was received to proceed with their recommended improvements over the following 6 weeks.

Sheet 1: Second-Level OEE Loss Analysis Sheet

The purpose of this sheet is to capture the loss data collected from Daily Production Reports and Team Observations so as to develop an "As-Is" situation for the Defined Production Area.

Capture the Continuous Recording Data (Spreadsheet 5.1)

Often the focus of the team is to conduct observations rather than try to capture as much information as possible through the Production Recording Process (daily production reports) during the 3-week data collection period (weeks 2–4).

As such, during the nominated data collection period (we suggest weeks 2, 3, and 4 of the cycle), it is important to capture as much detail as possible from the Daily Production Reports.

> *The exception to this is if there is a need to use a longer period to cover the majority of the product mix. For example, if you are running a 4-weekly Product Wheel, then you may need to extend the data collection period to 4 weeks; however, we would caution exceeding 4 weeks as the team may not have enough time to do a thorough analysis before their midway presentation typically at week 6 after their kick-off.*

Before starting this, the team should review the details of what is captured each day and determine whether this can be practically enhanced. For example, if the team has decided to divide the Production Area or Line into five sections (e.g., for a bottling line—Filler, Capper, Labeler, Packer, Palletizer), then the Daily Production Report may need to be reconfigured to allow Operators to easily record where their losses occur rather than just record the total loss (e.g., Filler downtime, Capper downtime, etc., rather than just Line downtime).

Any Planned Downtime should also be captured as per the agreed categories.

We would also suggest, for the nominated 3-week data collection period, a nominated team member, initially supported by the CI Coordinator, to make a habit of visiting the line at least just before the end of each shift to review the completeness of the data captured for the shift and discuss any anomalies with the Frontline Leader/Operators rather than wait for the end of the week to find that the data isn't as helpful as hoped for.

During this period, the High-Level OEE should continue to be measured (should have been started once the team kicked-off) and plotted on a run chart on a daily (24 hour) basis with the weekly average plotted on a weekly run chart. This should highlight if there are any cyclic trends relating to time of week or time of month.

The High-Level OEE run charts (daily and weekly) once established in week 2 should be an ongoing practice to allow monitoring of the impact of any improvements initiated during the cycle as well as future cycles. In later cycles, it will also become a means of monitoring whether Production Area Based Team improvement activity (Work Area Management/5S and the 7 Steps of Operator Equipment Management/Autonomous Maintenance) can be conducted each week because this activity is often dependent on an agreed upon level of OEE performance being achieved each week before the Production Area or Line can be stopped for the weekly improvement activity.

Spreadsheet 5.1

Second-Level OEE Loss Analysis	Loss Description	Baseline Analysis Previous 6 Weeks	"As-Is" OEE Loss Analysis (Typically Weeks 2–4 of the Cycle)						"As-Is" OEE	"As-Is" OEE
			Prod Reports (Week 2)	Prod Reports (Week 3)	Prod Reports (Week 4)	Ob 1 (Tue) (8:30–12:30) (Week 2)	Ob 2 (Wed) (10:30–2:30) (Week 3)	Ob 3 (Thu) (12:30–4:30) (Week 4)		
		% Loss	% Loss	% Loss	% Loss	% Loss	% Loss	% Loss	% Loss	% Loss
Planned Downtime	Planned Maintenance	3.0%	9.0%	0.0%	0.0%	0.0%	0.0%	0.0%	3.0%	
	Team Daily Review/Toolbox Meeting	2.0%	2.0%	2.0%	2.0%	0.0%	0.0%	2.0%	2.0%	
	Planned Start of Shift Downtime	1.0%	1.0%	1.0%	1.0%	0.0%	0.0%	1.0%	1.0%	
	Paid Breaks Downtime								0.0%	
	Planned End of Shift Downtime	1.0%	1.0%	1.0%	1.0%	0.0%	0.0%	1.0%	1.0%	
	WAM/OEM Activity Time								0.0%	
	Other Planned Downtime								0.0%	7.0%
Setup Downtime	Setup/Changeover Time	6.0%	6.5%	6.9%	7.0%	6.5%	0.0%	3.5%	6.8%	6.8%
Unplanned Recorded Downtime	Filler	10.5%	3.3%	2.8%	1.1%	1.1%	1.3%	1.2%	2.4%	
	Capper		4.2%	2.1%	2.7%	0.3%	2.6%	0.0%	3.0%	
	Labeler		1.9%	1.5%	2.3%	0.5%	0.0%	1.1%	1.9%	
	Packer		3.8%	2.2%	2.7%	0.4%	1.5%	0.0%	2.9%	
	Palletizer		2.1%	1.1%	2.5%	0.8%	0.7%	0.0%	1.9%	12.1%

A

(Continued)

Second-Level OEE Loss Analysis — Loss Description	Baseline Analysis Previous 6 Weeks % Loss	"As-Is" OEE Loss Analysis (Typically Weeks 2–4 of the Cycle)							"As-Is" OEE % Loss
		Prod Reports (Week 2) % Loss	Prod Reports (Week 3) % Loss	Prod Reports (Week 4) % Loss	Ob 1 (Tue) (8:30–12:30) (Week 2) % Loss	Ob 2 (Wed) (10:30–2:30) (Week 3) % Loss	Ob 3 (Thu) (12:30–4:30) (Week 4) % Loss	"As-Is" OEE % Loss	
Minor Unrecorded Stoppages — Filler					1.3%	1.8%	0.5%	1.2%	
Capper					0.5%	1.5%	0.1%	0.7%	
Labeler					1.0%	0.5%	0.9%	0.8%	
Packer					1.2%	2.1%	0.9%	1.4%	
Palletizer					0.5%	0.7%	0.9%	0.7%	**4.8%**
Slow Running		13.2%	12.9%	10.2%	1.6%	0.2%	2.3%	1.4%	
R **Reduced Speed** — Time to achieve Good Output at Correct Speed after start-up (e.g., from a setup or breakdown)					6.0%	0.0%	2.5%	2.8%	**4.2%**

(Continued)

"As-Is" OEE Loss Analysis (Typically Weeks 2–4 of the Cycle)

Second-Level OEE Loss Analysis		Loss Description	Baseline Analysis Previous 6 Weeks	Prod Reports (Week 2)	Prod Reports (Week 3)	Prod Reports (Week 4)	Ob 1 (Tue) (8:30–12:30) (Week 2)	Ob 2 (Wed) (10:30–2:30) (Week 3)	Ob 3 (Thu) (12:30–4:30) (Week 4)	"As-Is" OEE	"As-Is" OEE
			% Loss	% Loss	% Loss	% Loss	% Loss	% Loss	% Loss	% Loss	% Loss
	Rejects and Rework	Filler		0.0%	0.3%	1.2%	0.9%	0.9%	0.7%	0.7%	
		Capper		0.1%	0.2%	0.3%	0.0%	0.9%	0.4%	0.3%	
		Labeler	1.5%	0.4%	0.5%	0.9%	0.5%	0.4%	0.9%	0.6%	2.3%
		Packer		0.5%	0.3%	1.0%	0.6%	0.4%	0.8%	0.6%	
Q		Palletizer		0.0%	0.2%	0.1%	0.1%	0.1%	0.1%	0.1%	
	Start-up and Yield Loss	Start-up Product Loss till Good Output		Unknown	Unknown	Unknown	2.9%	0.0%	1.3%	1.4%	2.8%
		Overfill Yield Loss while running		Unknown	Unknown	Unknown	1.3%	1.4%	1.5%	1.4%	
		Error in Data Collection	17.0%	n/a	n/a	n/a	0.0%	0.0%	0.0%	n/a	
		Total Losses (Potential for Improvement)	42.0%	49.0%	35.0%	36.0%	28.0%	17.0%	23.6%	40.0%	40.0%
		HLOEE	58.0%	51.0%	65.0%	64.0%	72.0%	83.0%	76.4%	60.0%	
		Production Reports Average HLOEE	60.0%								

We often find that Operators (especially those involved in the improvement team) are happy to put the extra effort in to capture the losses as accurately as possible for a short period on the basis that it is being used by the improvement team to assist with reducing their frustrations and they receive regular feedback on their efforts (e.g., daily chats and weekly briefing) in front of the improvement team scoreboard where the information collected is displayed (daily and weekly High-Level OEE Run Charts along with any Loss Analysis Sheets and any Pareto Analysis).

Conduct Observations

Observations are an important part of OEE Loss Analysis. They allow the team to assess the accuracy of the Continuous Recording Data, collect minor unrecorded stoppages, identify unplanned interventions, and gain feedback from the Operators regarding possible improvement opportunities.

An observation sheet should be developed by the improvement team using the Sample OEE Observation Sheet template as a guide. The Observation Sheet should be divided into the sections decided for the Production Area or Line, or have a sheet for each section.

Sample OEE Observation Sheet

Production Area or Line:			Team Name:	Date:	
Sections Covered[a]:		Product(s) Run:	Product Spec Notes:	Sheet of Observer:	
Start Time	Finish Time	Remarks/Comments		First-Level Pareto Code	Possible Wording for Second-Level Pareto

[a] As per the Second-Level OEE Loss Analysis Sheet

Codes	First-Level Pareto	Other Information Required during Observation Period (Suggest this is collected by the CI Coordinator over the sampling period [hence needs to be there at the start and finish])	
001	Planned Downtime	Total Elapsed Time of Measurement Period	Minutes
002	Setup or Changeover Downtime	Total Amount Processed (or Amount Input)	(Units)
003	Unplanned Recorded Downtime (by Operator)	Total Rejects & Rework	(Units)
004	Minor Unrecorded Stoppages (as defined)	Good Output (first pass) Produced	(Units)
		Actual Production Speed (or cycle time) measure for a short time (e.g., 1–5 minute)	Units/ minute
A	Special Events Time	Ideal Speed (as per agreed upon definition)	Units/ minute
B	No Production Required Time	Copy of Operator Log Sheet (or Control Systems Logs) for measurement period	Yes/No
		Copy of any Quality Check Sheets for the measurement period	Yes/No

OEE SAMPLING THROUGH OBSERVATIONS

Who: All team members apart from the Operators who should be operating the equipment when the sample is carried out.

How long: Normally, we allocate 1 hour to each available team member on a relay approach. For example, if you have five team members available and the production area or line can be observed by one person, you would do a 5-hour continuous observation with each team member being present for 1 hour.

How do we qualify our Observations: Discuss the results with the Operators. If they say the results are abnormal, then repeat the observation during a different time frame.

If the team members have not been involved in an OEE Observation before, it is recommended they do a sample observation involving all team members to check the appropriateness of the sheet or sheets before the actual observation occurs (suggest a 30-minute event for the team with 5–10 minute briefing in front of the line or equipment to be observed to ensure everyone knows what is expected, a 15-minute observation, then a 5–10 minute debriefing to analyze the figures and confirm a standard approach for all to adopt).

At some sites where it is impractical to quickly take the improvement team to the line or equipment for the sample observation, a 15-minute video of the actual line or equipment is created and used for the sample observation.

During the 15-minute observation, the CI Coordinator should collect the "Other Information Required" in the bottom right-hand box of the OEE Observation Sheet.

The first Observation should be taken during week 2, followed by a second in week 3, and, if needed, a third in week 4. Always check after each observation whether the Operators running the line felt this was a representative or typical period of operation or whether there were unusual circumstances (or special causes affecting performance). Preferably, the observations should be taken over different time frames to hopefully capture different activities during the shifts.

Undertake Observations ideally one in weeks 2, 3, and 4. A minimum of two observations should be conducted with each Observer specifically capturing the following:

- Minor Unrecorded Stoppages
- Any evidence of speed slowdowns
- Operator interventions or frustrations (ask them)

It is important that the CI Coordinator captures sufficient information at the start and finish of each Observation (refer to the Other Information Required section of the Observation Sheet) so that a High-Level OEE can be calculated and hence used to verify whether there were any gaps in the other information collected.

The outcome from each Observation should be recorded on the Second-Level OEE Loss Analysis Sheet recognizing that any Speed Loss or Start-up and Yield Loss will have to be calculated using the appropriate equations to work out their percent impact on OEE (also refer to Chapter 3 for use of the equations) (Figure 5.1).

Reduced Speed Losses (typically rounded to closest minute):

$$\frac{\text{Net Production Time (minutes)} \times [\text{Ideal Speed (units/minute)} - \text{Actual Speed (units/minute)}]}{\text{Ideal speed (units/minute)}}$$

Rejects and Rework Losses (typically rounded to closest minute):

$$\frac{\text{Total Rejects and Rework (units)}}{\text{Ideal Speed (units/minute)}}$$

Start-up and Yield Losses (typically rounded to closest minute):

$$\frac{\text{Total Start-up and Yield Loss (units)}}{\text{Ideal Speed (units/minute)}}$$

Figure 5.1   Equations to assist calculating OEE using the Time Loss approach.

Populate the Second-Level OEE Loss Analysis Sheet

Each week, populate the relevant yellow parts of the Second-Level OEE Loss Analysis Sheet starting with the High-Level OEE figure for the week and then adding the Production Reported losses. Any discrepancies between the High-Level OEE and the Production Reported losses will be shown as Rate Loss.

After each Observation, populate the relevant yellow and green parts of the Second-Level OEE Loss Analysis Sheet starting with the High-Level OEE figure for the Observation. If there is any discrepancy in the losses observed and the High-Level OEE, it will be shown as Error in Data Collection. If this figure is significant, then further observations should be conducted to identify the cause for the discrepancy.

Once at least 3 weeks of Production Reports including the weekly High-Level OEE figure and two good Observations (hopefully three) have been entered on the sheet, the "As-Is OEE" will be automatically calculated using the data in the yellow section of the sheet.

Ideally, the "As-Is" OEE is very close to the Production Reports Average High-Level OEE. If there is a significant discrepancy, then further analysis is required to determine the cause.

This is typically done by using the Production Report Data for Planned Downtime, Setup Downtime, Unplanned Recorded Downtime, and Rejects & Rework provided the Observation Data does not highlight any great anomalies, and using the Observation Data for Minor Unrecorded Stoppages, Reduced Speed, Rejects and Rework, and Start-up and Yield Loss recognizing that Rejects and Rework is the only loss taken from both sources of data.

Reduced Speed can involve two components:

■ Slow Running
■ Time to achieve Good Output at Correct Speed after start-up following setup or breakdown or start of shift if line stops

Slow Running loss should be recorded by the CI Coordinator at least at the start of the Observation and before the conclusion of the Observation (if time permits, a few more checks could be helpful) using 2- to 5-minute samples, with the result averaged for the Observation.

Reduced Speed % Loss should be calculated using the equation in the previous page (also refer to Chapter 3 for use of the equation).

Time to achieve Good Output at Correct Speed should be any difference between Reduced Speed and Slow Running.

Rejects & Rework % Loss (assuming there has been a physical count of rejects and rework) should be calculated using the equation in the previous page (also refer to Chapter 3 for use of the equation).

Start-up & Yield % Loss (assuming there has been a physical count of Start-up losses and Yield Loss) should be calculated using the equation in the previous page (also refer to Chapter 3 for use of the equation).

The key is to gain consensus by the team that the "As-Is" OEE is as good as can be reasonably assessed.

Note: Expect the High-Level OEE (HLOEE) for "As Is" to be higher than Baseline HLOEE. This is normal and is often a consequence of the Hawthorne effect (improved performance owing to attention in area).

Sheet 2: Second-Level OEE Loss Summary Sheet

The purpose of this sheet is to interpret the initial OEE Loss Data using Pareto charts.

The data from the Second-Level OEE Loss Analysis is used to automatically create a Summary Table by Section and Loss Type to allow the creation of the First-Level Total Loss Pareto by Section and the First-Level Loss Pareto by Loss Type. This helps identify if there is a particular Section of the Production Area or Line that is causing the most losses or whether a particular Loss Type is having significant impact on OEE performance.

In the example presented, the Section losses of "Across the Line" are most significant, followed by the Packer, whereas the Loss Type that is most significant is Unplanned Recorded Downtime.

The Second-Level OEE Loss Summary also has provision to include the distribution of manning for the line to see if a particular manning position is generating more losses than other positions (Spreadsheet 5.2a).

Spreadsheet 5.2a

Second-Level OEE Loss Summary Sheet

Section	Manning	A			R		Q		Total Loss	People Allocation
		Planned Downtime	Setup Downtime	Unplanned Recorded Downtime	Minor Unrecorded Stoppages	Reduced Speed	Rejects and Rework	Start-up and Yield		
Filler	1			2.4%	1.2%		0.7%		**4.3%**	8.3%
Capper				3.0%	0.7%		0.3%		**4.0%**	
Labeler				1.9%	0.8%		0.6%		**3.3%**	10.9%
Packer	2			2.9%	1.4%		0.6%		**4.9%**	
Palletizer				1.9%	0.7%		0.1%		**2.7%**	
Across the Line	1	7.0%	6.8%			4.2%		2.8%	**20.8%**	20.8%
Totals	**4**	**7.0%**	**6.8%**	**12.1%**	**4.8%**	**4.2%**	**2.3%**	**2.8%**	**40.0%**	
OEE									**60.0%**	

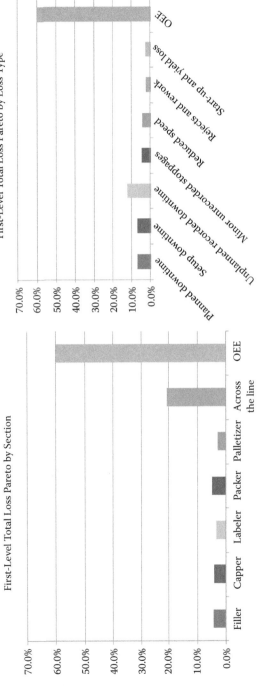

First-Level Total Loss Pareto by Loss Type

First-Level Total Loss Pareto by Section

Spreadsheet 5.2b

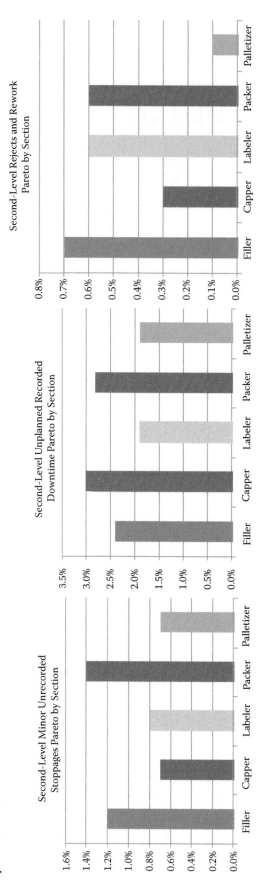

To further the analysis, Second-Level Pareto charts by Section are also generated to identify which Sections are generating specific Loss Types (Spreadsheet 5.2b).

In the example presented, initial possible opportunities could be for a Setup Time Reduction team to be established to address the 6.8% Loss, and a Micro Focused Equipment & Process Improvement team to be established to address the 4.9% losses at the Packer.

Sheet 3: First-Level OEE Loss Analysis Sheet

The purpose of this sheet is to summarize the data collected in the Second-Level OEE Loss Analysis to make it simpler to present to the CI Leadership Team and other people working in the area if required. This sheet is automatically populated from all the data entered into the Second-Level OEE Loss Analysis Sheet (Spreadsheet 5.3).

Sheet 4: Second-Level OEE Improvement Visions Sheet

This sheet is typically created during Step 4 of the Macro Focused Equipment & Process Improvement Process. Its purpose is to develop an Ideal Vision and 12-Month Vision with supporting reasons/assumptions for approval by the CI Leadership Team.

We populate the "As-Is" OEE Columns directly from the Second-Level OEE Loss Analysis Sheet.

We then populate the Ideal Vision within 3 years column line by line with the reason or assumption noted in the adjoining column (Spreadsheet 5.4).

A key learning has been that many sites take a "good enough" approach to setting their 3-year Ideal OEE Vision rather than like Toyota's strive for "perfection" approach and set a vision on perfect performance within the constraints of current working arrangements at the site.

The OEE Improvement Visions Sheet should be seen as a management training tool to demonstrate the importance of striving for "perfection" (True North) rather than "good enough."

The concept of "perfection" as referred to on numerous occasions by Jeffrey K. Liker in his book *The Toyota Way for Lean Leadership* is probably best described on page 94 when he says: "Not fixing the root cause may be acceptable for ***good enough***, but it doesn't fly in a quest for ***perfection***."

The OEE Improvement Visions Sheet is also based on the principles of Zero-Based budgeting. In other words, forget what previous performance and targets were. Look to the new learning of what future Production Area Based Team improvement activities of Work Area Management/5S and the 7 Steps of Operator Equipment Management/Autonomous Maintenance can achieve for the

Spreadsheet 5.3

First-Level OEE Loss Analysis — Loss Description		Baseline Analysis Previous 6 Weeks % Loss	"As-Is" OEE Loss Analysis (Typically Weeks 2–4 of the Cycle)						
			Prod Reports (Week 2) % Loss	Prod Reports (Week 3) % Loss	Prod Reports (Week 4) % Loss	Ob 1 (Tue) (8:30–12:30) (Week 2) % Loss	Ob 2 (Wed) (10:30–2:30) (Week 3) % Loss	Ob 3 (Thu) (12:30–4:30) (Week 4) % Loss	"As-Is" OEE % Loss
A	**Planned Downtime**	7.0%	13.0%	4.0%	4.0%	0.0%	0.0%	4.0%	7.0%
	Setup Downtime	6.0%	6.5%	6.9%	7.0%	6.5%	0.0%	3.5%	6.8%
	Unplanned Recorded Downtime	10.5%	15.3%	9.7%	11.3%	3.1%	6.1%	2.3%	12.1%
R	**Minor Unrecorded Stoppages**	0.0%	13.2%	12.9%	10.2%	4.5%	6.6%	3.3%	4.8%
	Reduced Speed	0.0%				7.6%	0.2%	4.8%	4.2%
Q	**Rejects and Rework**	1.5%	1.0%	1.5%	3.5%	2.1%	2.7%	2.9%	2.3%
	Start-up and Yield Loss	0.0%	0.0%	0.0%	0.0%	4.2%	1.4%	2.8%	2.8%
	Error in Data Collection	17.0%							
	Total Losses (Potential for Improvement)	42.0%	49.0%	35.0%	36.0%	28.0%	17.0%	23.6%	40.0%
	OEE	58.0%	51.0%	65.0%	64.0%	72.0%	83.0%	76.4%	60.0%

Spreadsheet 5.4

Second-Level OEE Improvement Visions / Loss Description		"As-Is" OEE % Loss	12 Mth Vision within 3 Cycles % Loss	Ideal Vision within 3 Years % Loss	Reasons/Assumptions for Ideal Vision within 3 Years/10 Cycles after Successfully Completing WAM/5S and the 7 Steps of Operator Equipment Management/Autonomous Maintenance	"As-Is" OEE % Loss	12 Month Vision within 3 Cycles % Loss	Ideal Vision within 3 Years % Loss
A Planned Downtime	Planned Maintenance	3.0%	0.0%	0.0%	To be incorporated into WAM/OEM activities			
	Team Daily Review/Toolbox Meeting	2.0%	2.0%	2.0%	10 minutes start of each shift			
	Planned Start of Shift Downtime	1.0%	1.0%	1.0%	10 minutes at start of dayshift			
	Paid Breaks Downtime	0.0%	0.0%	0.0%	Hot seat line so always running			
	Planned End of Shift Downtime	1.0%	1.0%	1.0%	10 minute at end of A/S to run out line			
	WAM/OEM Activity Time	0.0%	5.0%	4.0%	1.6 hour per shift per week			
	Other Planned Downtime	0.0%	0.0%	0.0%		7.0%	9.0%	8.0%
Setup Downtime	Setup/Changeover Time	6.8%	4.6%	2.5%	10 product changeovers per week with an allowance of 12 minute per changeover	6.8%	4.6%	2.5%
Unplanned Recorded Downtime	Filler	2.4%	1.3%	2.0%	Goal is zero breakdowns; however, will allow 2% or 10 minute per shift	12.1%	6.8%	2.0%
	Capper	3.0%	1.8%					
	Labeler	1.9%	1.1%					
	Packer	2.9%	1.6%					
	Palletizer	1.9%	1.0%					

(Continued)

Second-Level OEE Improvement Visions

Loss Description		"As-Is" OEE % Loss	12 Month Vision within 3 Cycles % Loss	Ideal Vision within 3 Years % Loss	Reasons/Assumptions for Ideal Vision within 3 Years/10 Cycles after Successfully Completing WAM/5S and the 7 Steps of Operator Equipment Management/Autonomous Maintenance	"As-Is" OEE % Loss	12 Month Vision within 3 Cycles % Loss	Ideal Vision within 3 Years % Loss
Minor Unrecorded Stoppages	Filler	1.2%	0.6%	0.0%	Goal is zero breakdowns; also we will be recording any minor stops so they will be recorded as unplanned recorded downtime for which there is an allowance	4.8%	2.6%	0.0%
	Capper	0.7%	0.4%					
	Labeler	0.8%	0.4%					
	Packer	1.4%	0.8%					
	Palletizer	0.7%	0.4%					
Reduced Speed (R)	Slow running	1.4%	0.7%	0.0%	Aim is to run Filler at Ideal Speed of 1,000 bottles per minute	4.2%	2.4%	1.0%
	Time to achieve good output at correct speed after start-up (e.g., from a setup or breakdown)	2.8%	1.7%	1.0%	Allow 5 minute to stabilize line after each changeover			
Rejects and Rework	Filler	0.7%	0.4%	0.6%	Rejects and rework due to breakdowns will be eliminated with goal of zero breakdowns; however, assume we will achieve a 70% improvement in quality, and hence allow 30% of current 2% = 0.6%	2.3%	1.2%	0.6%
	Capper	0.3%	0.2%					
	Labeler	0.6%	0.3%					
	Packer	0.6%	0.3%					
	Palletizer	0.1%	0.0%					
Start-up and Yield Loss (Q)	Start-up product loss till good output	1.4%	1.2%	0.9%	Based on 3 minute flush at start of dayshift and after each changeover (15 events per week)	2.8%	2.4%	1.9%
	Overfill yield loss while running	1.4%	1.2%	1.0%	Due to accuracy of current filler need to allow 1%			
Total Losses (Potential for Improvement)		**40.0%**	**29.0%**	**16.0%**		40.0%	29.0%	16.0%
OEE		**60.0%**	**71.0%**	**84.0%**				

Production Area or Line that is also being improved by everyone being involved in ongoing Cross-functional Team improvement. The aim is to specify what each of the 7 OEE losses "could be" supported by clear assumptions/explanations so as to achieve "perfect" performance.

As the 3-year Ideal Vision part of the OEE Improvement Visions Sheet is presented to the CI Leadership Team, it should be used as a training tool to reinforce the concept of "perfection" versus "good enough." For this reason, ideally the first few OEE Improvement Visions Sheets should be presented to the CI Leadership Team by a CI Specialist as a training activity before the Macro Focused Equipment & Process Improvement Team presents it at their Midway and Final Presentations. Later, this should be the role of the CI Coordinator to present.

Note: *When establishing your Ideal Vision, consider the following:*

- *Planned Downtime will often be influenced by the current employee contract or enterprise agreement regarding breaks, clean-up time, and so on.*
- *Unplanned Downtime will be dependent on the nature of the plant; however, typically it should be set around 1%–3%. Some 20 years ago, International Maintenance Benchmarking identified that <3% was Best Practice for manufacturing industries, whereas it was set at 0% for Aircraft and the Nuclear industry.*
- *Minor Unrecorded Stoppages should be zero as all stoppages should be getting recorded.*
- *Rejects and Rework should be set around 0.5%–0%.*
- *Setup Downtime and Start-up & Yield Losses will be dependent on the business requirements for product changes and the process of the changeover; however, it is worth noting that under the concept of SMED (Single Minute Exchange of Dies), the target for all setups or changeovers should be below 10 minutes, and under Toyota's guidelines, the total setup time loss should not exceed 10%.*

Next, we would fill in the 12-Month Vision within the 3 Cycles column, which is designed to set a vision for the Production Area or Line.

This should be based on the understanding that the impact of the improvement journey is exponential, with the Production Area or Line typically achieving 50% of the Ideal Vision within 1 year and the other 50% over the following 2 years. This is mainly attributed to the first year focusing on the "low-hanging fruit" and the remaining 2 years continually chasing the smaller incremental improvements.

The Second-Level OEE Improvement Visions Sheet should be presented to the CI Leadership Team before the Midway Presentation by the CI Specialist or CI Coordinator to gain their agreement on the assumptions used for the Ideal Vision.

Sheet 5: Second-Level OEE Improvement Gap High-Level Opportunity Analysis Sheet

The purpose of this sheet is to identify what sort of team will best address each Loss Gap so that the CI Leadership Team can determine the need for Production Area Based Team improvement activities of Work Area Management/5S and the 7 Steps of Operator Equipment Management/Autonomous Maintenance (Spreadsheet 5.5).

We populate the first two columns ("As-Is" OEE; Ideal Vision within 3 Years) directly from the Second-Level OEE Loss Improvement Visions Sheet.

The Gap Analysis column should be automatically generated as it is the difference between the "As-Is" and the Ideal Vision.

The issue to be addressed next is where does the improvement effort lie? Is it best addressed by Cross-functional Team or Production Area Based Team improvements?

Our learning has been that Technical issues tend to be best addressed by Cross-functional Teams and People Development issues are best addressed by Production Area Based Team improvement activity such as Work Area Management/5S and the 7 Steps of Operator Equipment Management/ Autonomous Maintenance.

To help make this a little clearer, let us use the example of a spring breaking on a machine causing the output to go out of specification.

The spring breaking is typically classified as a Technical issue in that the spring may not be strong enough for the application, or the Preventive/Predictive Maintenance Plan may not be effective enough to pick on the need to replace the spring before it fails. Addressing the need for an improved spring might require a Cross-functional Team involving a Design Engineer to specify spring parameters, a Maintenance person to ensure that the new spring will be easy to maintain and wherever possible be of a common or standard type already being used on site, an Operator to ensure that the new design will be easy to access for cleaning and or checking, and a Quality person to ensure that any change will not affect the quality requirements of the output.

Alternatively, you could have the situation where the spring is allowed to become corroded by poor operational practices (high-pressure water blasting to clean the machine) or weakened by contamination from the process, lodging in and around the spring, placing extra load on it.

When the spring breaks, you may also have the situation where the Operators don't immediately realize that it has broken and it is only after some time that they realize they are producing out-of-specification output and hence stop the machine to find the problem. Finding the problem may then take quite some time because they don't have a good understanding of the functioning of their machine and the Maintenance person may take some time to arrive at the Machine. All of these issues would be classified as People Development issues in that the people do not have the knowledge or skills to address the situation immediately.

Spreadsheet 5.5

Second-Level OEE Improvement Gap High Level Opportunity Analysis		"As-Is" OEE	Ideal Vision within 3 Years	Gap Analysis	High Level Opportunities Analysis		Gap Analysis	High Level Opportunity	
					Cross-Functional Teams (Technical)	Area Based Teams (People Development)		XFT	ABT
Loss Description		% Loss	% Loss	% Loss	% Loss	% Loss	% Loss	% Loss	% Loss
Planned Downtime	Planned Maintenance	3.0%	0.0%	3.0%	0.00%	3.00%			
	Team Daily Review/ Toolbox Meeting	2.0%	2.0%	0.0%					
	Planned Start of Shift Downtime	1.0%	1.0%	0.0%					
	Paid Breaks Downtime	0.0%	0.0%	0.0%					
	Planned End of Shift Downtime	1.0%	1.0%	0.0%					
	WAM/OEM Activity Time	0.0%	4.0%	-4.0%	0.00%	-4.00%	-1.0%	0.0%	-1.0%
	Other Planned Downtime	0.0%	0.0%	0.0%					
Setup Downtime	Setup/Changeover Time	6.8%	2.5%	4.3%	3.23%	1.07%	4.3%	3.2%	1.1%
Unplanned Recorded Downtime	Filler	2.4%	2.0%	2.0%	1.00%	1.00%			
	Capper	3.0%		2.6%	1.30%	1.30%			
	Labeler	1.9%		1.5%	0.75%	0.75%			
	Packer	2.9%		2.5%	1.25%	1.25%			
	Palletizer	1.9%		1.5%	0.75%	0.75%	10.1%	5.0%	5.1%

(Continued)

Second-Level OEE Improvement Gap High Level Opportunity Analysis

	Loss Description	"As-Is" OEE	Ideal Vision within 3 Years	Gap Analysis	High Level Opportunities Analysis		Gap Analysis	High Level Opportunity	
					Cross-Functional Teams (Technical)	Area Based Teams (People Development)		XFT	ABT
		% Loss	% Loss	% Loss	% Loss	% Loss	% Loss	% Loss	% Loss
R	**Minor Unrecorded Stoppages** — Filler	1.2%		1.2%	0.30%	0.90%			
	Capper	0.7%	0.0%	0.7%	0.18%	0.52%			
	Labeler	0.8%		0.8%	0.40%	0.40%			
	Packer	1.4%		1.4%	0.35%	1.05%	4.8%	1.4%	3.4%
	Palletizer	0.7%		0.7%	0.18%	0.52%			
	Slow Running	1.4%	0.0%	1.4%	0.35%	1.05%			
	Reduced Speed — Time to achieve Good Output at Correct Speed after start-up (e.g., from a setup or breakdown)	2.8%	1.0%	1.8%	0.90%	0.90%	3.2%	1.3%	1.9%
	Rejects and Rework — Filler	0.7%		0.5%	0.25%	0.25%			
	Capper	0.3%	0.6%	0.2%	0.10%	0.10%			
	Labeler	0.6%		0.5%	0.20%	0.30%			
	Packer	0.6%		0.5%	0.25%	0.25%			
	Palletizer	0.1%		0.0%	0.00%	0.00%	1.7%	0.8%	0.9%
Q	**Start-up and Yield Loss** — Start-up Product Loss till Good Output	1.4%	0.9%	0.5%	0.00%	0.50%			
	Overfill Yield Loss while running	1.4%	1.0%	0.4%	0.30%	0.10%	0.9%	0.3%	0.6%
	Total Losses (Potential for Improvement)	40.0%	16.0%	24.0%	12.0%	12.0%	24.0%	12.0%	12.0%
	OEE	60.0%	84.0%						

We suggest that you work through the Gap Analysis for each loss by asking the team to seek out what typically happened when the loss occurred. Why did it take so long to get going or why did we have the quantity of loss? The aim is not to search for the cause of the loss but rather to determine whether there are any People Development issues that increased the extent of the loss.

Example Situation:
When the spring broke, we kept running for 5 minutes before we realized we were making out-of-specification output (rejects). We called a fitter and it took 15 minutes to find the problem and then it was fixed in 10 minutes.

Example Assessment:
Based on the situation above, we could say 50% of the loss can be attributed to People Development Issues because we didn't have the knowledge and skill to identify the problem immediately and 50% can be attributed to Technical Issues because we may need a better spring or better PM system to pick up on replacing the spring before it breaks.

We find it helpful to divide each loss into 25% proportions, for example, the loss is best addressed by 25% Cross-functional Team activity and 75% Production Area Based Team activity or 50% and 50% or 75% and 25% or 0% and 100%. It is easy to set up such ratio formulas in the spreadsheet and apply the formulas based on the consensus of the team to the relevant columns.

Typically, when we sum up the percentages in the two columns, we find that the result is either approximately 50% Cross-functional Team activity to address the losses and approximately 50% Production Area Based Team activity to address the losses, or Production Area Based Team activity is higher than the Cross-functional Team activity because often the obvious Technical issues have already been addressed.

The key outcome from this activity is to justify to the CI Leadership Team the need for Production Area Based Team improvement activity involving Work Area Management/5S and the 7 Steps of Operator Equipment Management/ Autonomous Maintenance if the Ideal Vision has any chance of being achieved.

Sheet 6: Second-Level OEE Improvement Targets Sheet

This sheet is typically created during Step 5 of the Macro Focused Equipment & Process Improvement process. Its purpose is to capture where the team expects to achieve its mandated OEE improvement (Spreadsheet 5.6).

We populate the first column ("As-Is" OEE) directly from the Second-Level OEE Improvement Visions Sheet.

Part of the Macro Focused Equipment & Process Improvement Team's mandate is to improve OEE by a nominated percentage. Typically, this will be between 10% and 25% depending on the Baseline OEE (if OEE is, say, 50%, then

Spreadsheet 5.6

Second-Level OEE Improvement Targets	Loss Description	"As-Is" OEE % Loss	Target for the End of This Cycle % Loss	Target for the End of This Cycle First-Level Totals	Improvement for This Cycle % Loss	Target at Completion of Cycle Reasons for Setting Target Improvements	# Imp Sheets	Estimated Cost	Annualized Savings
	Planned Maintenance	3.0%	3.0%		0.0%				
	Team Daily Review/ Toolbox Meeting	2.0%	2.0%		0.0%				
	Planned Start of Shift Downtime	1.0%	1.0%		0.0%				
Planned Downtime	Paid Breaks Downtime	0.0%			0.0%				
	Planned End of Shift Downtime	1.0%	1.0%		0.0%				
	WAM/OEM Activity Time	0.0%			0.0%				
	Other Planned Downtime	0.0%		7.0%	0.0%				
Setup Downtime	Setup/Changeover Time	6.8%	5.6%	5.6%	1.2%	Improve storage of parts (10% improvement) Improve communications with Maintenance (10% improvement)	3		
	Filler	2.4%	2.4%		0.0%				
	Capper	3.0%	2.1%		0.9%	Improved feed of lids (30% improvement)	1	$3,620	$192,050
Unplanned Recorded Downtime	Labeler	1.9%	1.3%		0.6%	Correct Label Feeder (30% improvement)	1		
	Packer	2.9%	2.0%		0.9%	Maint to replace worn components (30% improvement)			
	Palletizer	1.9%	1.3%	9.1%	0.6%	Improve Stretch Wrap Tensioner (30% improvement)	1		

(Continued)

Second-Level OEE Improvement Targets / Loss Description		"As-Is" OEE % Loss	Target for the End of This Cycle % Loss	First-Level Totals	Improvement for This Cycle % Loss	Reasons for Setting Target Improvements	# Imp Sheets	Estimated Cost	Annualized Savings
R	**Minor Unrecorded Stoppages**	Filler	1.2%	1.2%		0.0%				
		Capper	0.7%	0.5%		0.2%	Improved feed of lids (50% improvement)		see above	see above
		Labeler	0.8%	0.4%		0.4%	Correct Label Feeder (50% improvement)			
		Packer	1.4%	1.0%		0.4%	Maint to replace worn components (30% improvement)			
		Palletizer	0.7%	0.5%	3.6%	0.2%	Improve Stretch Wrap Tensioner (50% improvement)			
	Reduced Speed	Slow Running	1.4%	1.30%		0.1%	Clearer understanding of expectations by Operators (5%)			
		Time to achieve Good Output at Correct Speed after start-up (e.g., from a setup or breakdown)	2.8%	2.8%	4.1%	0.0%				
Q	**Rejects and Rework**	Filler	0.7%	0.8%		−1.0%				
		Capper	0.3%	0.2%		0.1%	Improved feed of lids (30% improvement)		see above	see above
		Labeler	0.6%	0.4%		0.2%	Correct Label Feeder (30% improvement)			
		Packer	0.6%	0.4%		0.2%	Maint to replace worn components (30% improvement)			
		Palletizer	0.1%	0.0%	1.8%	0.1%				
	Start-up and Yield Loss	Start-up Product Loss till Good Output	1.4%	1.4%		0.0%				
		Overfill Yield Loss while running	1.4%	1.4%	2.8%	0.0%				
Total Losses (Potential for Improvement)			**40.0%**	**34.0%**	**34.0%**	**6.0%**		6	$3,620	$192,050
OEE			60.0%	66.0%	66.0%	66.0%				
							% **Improvement to "As-Is":**	10%		

the initial target would typically be 25%, whereas if the Baseline OEE was 70%, then the initial target would typically be 10%).

This sheet allows the team to summarize their expected outcomes from their possible root causes and solutions to improve OEE. It hopefully identifies where and why they believe they can achieve or exceed the nominated OEE improvement target.

An important thing to remember when identifying possible impact of improvements is that losses are not unique and are usually related to each other. Hence, sometimes it is helpful to group the losses into the designated areas or sections where appropriate.

For example: Filler "As-Is" losses = 2.4% + 1.2% + 0.8% = 4.4% because when the Filler is unreliable, we usually incur not just Unplanned Recorded Downtime and Minor Unrecorded Stoppages but also Rejects & Rework and Speed Losses through slowdown and start-ups. (Note: we haven't allocated the speed losses at this stage as it is often too difficult to identify.)

When selecting possible losses (Pareto charting can be of assistance here) for improvement during the cycle, it should be remembered that Cross-functional teams (e.g., Micro Focused Equipment & Process Improvement Team focusing on a Section) are best to address the Technical issues and to leave the People Development issues to the Production Area Based Teams.

Warning: *Don't be tempted at this point now that losses have been indentified to target the highest % Loss first. We need to ask what the true cost of each loss is. What are the highest cost losses? As such, in most situations, the Quality-related losses will bring more gain to the business in that they will not only improve OEE but also reduce material costs in many cases.*

Once the losses to be improved in this cycle are identified, populate the Improvement for this Cycle column along with the Reason for Setting Target Improvements column.

Sheet 7: Production Area or Line Cost–Benefit Sheet

The purpose of this sheet is to determine the cost and benefit from each proposed improvement.

Section:	Capper
Improvement:	Improved feed of lids (30% improvement)
Impact:	OEE increase by 0.9 + 0.2 + 0.1 = 1.2%

(Continued)

Assumptions:	Line is crewed for 2 shifts × 8 hours × 5 days × 50 weeks a year
	Extra good output cannot be sold in the short term, so line will finish early once production plan achieved
	Ideal Speed of Line is 1000 bottles per minute
	Cost of Contents of Bottle is $0.30
	Cost of Lost Bottle (Scrap) is $0.80

As each improvement is identified, it can be costed using the Production Area or Line Cost–Benefit template, which should be created by the CI Leadership Team and given to the team at the start of their cycle. The figures in yellow do not have to be exact, but rather rounded figures that the CI Leadership Team is happy to make decisions on (Spreadsheet 5.7).

Once all the proposed improvements have been costed and their benefits calculated, the summary information can be entered on the Second-Level OEE Improvements Target Sheet.

Sheet 8: First-Level OEE Improvement Summary Sheet

This sheet is typically created during Step 8 of the Macro Focused Equipment & Process Improvement Process. Its purpose is to summarize the analysis for the Team's Final Presentation and should be available for review and approval by the CI Leadership Team before the Pre-cycle Strategy Planning Session (typically 2 weeks before the end of the cycle to determine next cycle teams) and team Final Presentation at the end of the cycle.

This sheet should be generated automatically from the previous sheets (Spreadsheet 5.8).

Key points from above:

■ If you only do Cross-functional Team improvement activities, the high likelihood is that OEE will only increase to 72%.
■ If you only do Prod Area Based Team improvement activities, the high likelihood is that OEE will only increase to 72%.
■ If you focus on both ongoing Cross-functional Team and Prod Area Based Team improvement, the high likelihood is that OEE will increase to 84%.

Spreadsheet 5.7

Production Area or Line Cost/Benefit Template		*Units*	*Rate*	*Quantity*	*$*
Cost of Improvement	1 Materials	$			$3,000
	2 Labor – Normal Time (approx)	$/hour	$30.00	10	$300
	3 Labor – Weekend Work (approx)	$/hour	$40.00	8	$320
	4 Outside Suppliers (e.g., special contractor)	$			
				Total Cost (A):	**$3,620**
		Units	*Rate*	*Quantity per Week*	*$*
Benefit from Improvement	1 Reduced Scrap (0.1% or 4.8 minutes)	$/unit	$0.80	4800	$3,840
	2 Reduced Rework Labor Cost – Normal Time	$/hour	$30.00		$0
	3 Reduced Rework Labor Cost – Overtime	$/hour	$40.00		$0
	4 Production Labor saving – Normal Time	$/hour	$30.00		$0
	5 Production Labor saving – Overtime	$/hour	$40.00		$0
	6 Energy Saving – Machinery (1.1% or 52 minutes)	$/hour	$1.00	0.88	$1
	7 Energy Saving – Lighting	$/hour	$0.25		$0
	8 Other Savings				
				Total Savings per week (B):	**$3,841**
	Payback Period (weeks)			**A divided by B: (weeks)**	0.9
	Weeks Worked per Year:				50.0
	Annualized Savings:			**B × Weeks worked per Year:**	**$192,050**

Spreadsheet 5.8

First-Level OEE Improvement Summary		"As-Is" OEE	Target for This Cycle	12 Month Vision within 3 Cycles	Ideal Vision within 3 Years	Gap Analysis	Opportunities Analysis	
Loss Description		% Loss	% Loss	% Loss	% Loss	% Loss	Cross-Functional Teams (Technical)	Area Based Teams (People Development)
	Planned Downtime	7.0%	7.0%	9.0%	8.0%	–1.0%	0.0%	–1.0%
A	Setup Downtime	6.8%	5.6%	4.6%	2.5%	4.3%	3.2%	1.1%
	Unplanned Recorded Downtime	12.1%	9.1%	6.8%	2.0%	10.1%	5.0%	5.1%
R	Minor Unrecorded Stoppages	4.8%	3.6%	2.6%	0.0%	4.8%	1.4%	3.4%
	Reduced Speed	4.2%	4.1%	2.4%	1.0%	3.2%	1.3%	1.9%
Q	Rejects and Rework	2.3%	1.8%	1.2%	0.6%	1.7%	0.8%	0.9%
	Start-up and Yield Loss	2.8%	2.8%	2.4%	1.9%	0.9%	0.3%	0.6%
Total Losses (Potential for Improvement)		40.0%	34.0%	29.0%	16.0%	24.0%	12.0%	12.0%
OEE		60.0%	66.0%	71.0%	84.0%		72.0%	72.0%

Key Learnings from Chapter 5

- The OEE Loss Analysis Spreadsheet consists of eight linked sheets.
- It is important to investigate both Total Loss by Section and Total Loss by Loss Type.
- Creating an Ideal Vision is designed to challenge current practices and reinforce what should be possible if Production Area Based Team Improvement activities are properly implemented.
- Using a Cost–Benefit Template created by the CI Leadership Team simplifies the justification process for improvements.
- The OEE Loss Analysis process should be repeated each 12 months for the Production Area or Line in order to monitor progress/achievements and set a new plan for the next 12 months.

Chapter 6

Automating OEE Data Capture

There are many options to automating OEE (Overall Equipment Effectiveness) data capture; some are very specifically focused on OEE while others tend to integrate a number of measurement tools such as SPC (Statistical Process Control), FMEA (Failure Mode & Effect Analysis), and OEE. Like most software applications, it is how you set them up and input into them that has the biggest impact on the value you gain.

Provided the software has been around for a number of years with some good supporting case studies and has the display and reporting features required, it will probably be satisfactory. It then becomes an issue of cost and support.

Too often, we have seen the same software used at different sites with vastly different outcomes, which again reinforces the need to focus on how you intend to set up and use the software.

When Should We Automate?

Our CTPM Improvement Toolbox hopefully provides the answer to this question (Figure 6.1).

"Don't Automate before Simplifying" provides sound advice like the advice from one software supplier: "never automate a mess"; otherwise, "you get an automated mess."

We have found that if OEE is low and there are a lot of losses, especially small losses, then it is very hard for Operators to capture all the losses accurately while they are rightfully focused on producing the required output.

An Operator once explained during one of our workshops that her General Manager was attending that, at the start of the shift, they (all the Operators) would be focused on recording the required data; however, if things started to go wrong, which often happened, they would focus on getting things working properly, and then when things settled down, they would go back to the production report and "give it their best guess" as to where all the time went and why!

Start at the left (Analysis), progressively move to the right (Automation)

Analysis	Simplification	Control	Automation
• Product analysis	• Product rationalization	• Dominant product flow	• ERP
• People/structure analysis	• Area based teams with frontline leaders	• Visual controls	• MRPII
• Measurement analysis	• Goal aligned measures	• Mistake proofing	• CMMS
• OEE analysis	• Loss reduction	• Pull systems	• Loss data
• Lead time analysis*	• Lead time reduction	• Kanbans	•
• Cost analysis	• Process stability	• Standards	•
	• Standardized work	• Compliance audits	•
*Includes value stream mapping		• Statistical process control (SPC)	

Key Learning: Don't Automate before Simplifying

Figure 6.1 CTPM Improvement Toolbox.

The General Manager, although looking rather surprised at the comment, soon understood where they were coming from and agreed with their actions, recognizing that the priority was to get the product to the correct quality and out the door.

We have found that by doing the detailed OEE Loss Analysis outlined in Chapter 5, and implementing a number of improvements, apart from gaining more capacity and reducing costs, you are generating more time for the Operators to more accurately capture loss data.

What Should Be Considered When Selecting the Software?

1. Accessibility

When researching this chapter, we spoke to several software suppliers. One supplier used by several of our clients is OFS (Operations Feedback System) (www.ofsystems.com), which believes that when it comes to software, the most important thing is accessibility.

In simple terms, this means that the intended user audience actually can competently use the tool, and even better, like using the tool. To have someone like a tool, you need up-front buy-in, which means they have a good understanding as to why the tool is important and find it is very easy to use. This can be covered by having excellent speed, comfort in operation, familiarity with tabs and commands, relevant content, attractive eye-catching screens, and, where possible, fun.

Without this, usage can be poor, resulting in poor outcomes. The trouble with lots of software purchases is that the buyers are often not the users, so this important step is often overlooked.

In practical terms, many organizations give ownership over OEE to engineering, so engineers go out and buy software they can use and then dump it into the hands of operations. The result is often poor usage and subsequent outcomes.

A clear example of this was immediately apparent when we started working with a large pharmaceutical company. They had spent considerable time and money developing an in-house information capture system with terminals at each line. Functionally, it was very good, with just about every bit of information regarding production on the system; however, we observed the following:

1. Nobody on the shopfloor really seemed to know how to use it.
2. When someone did try to use it, it was extremely slow and hence not very helpful.

When they initiated two Cross-functional improvement teams to focus on two lines to improve OEE performances, it became obvious that the current in-house system, although an absolute fountain of knowledge for those with the capability and patience to use it, was not up to the task. So they decided to install OFS on one of the lines as a trial because of its very user-friendly nature, as well as affordability. After their 12-week cycle, the results from the team that had access to OFS were more than double that of the other team. In the team's final presentation, they stated that their results were attributed to the easy accessibility of data that helped them pinpoint where to focus their improvement.

2. Information Design

Developing an OEE Data Capture Model is a great starting point. From a Continuous Improvement perspective, loss data capture should, apart from duration, have at least five main fields: loss, code, location, type, and reason.

Some companies want to make this an enterprise policy so that each site in the enterprise is calling the same loss the same thing so that sharing of learning between sites is easier. That is why developing the OEE definitions outlined in Chapter 2 is so important before automating your OEE data capture. However, the challenge you have in developing an enterprise policy for OEE loss reasons is that there can be a tendency for sites to start comparing their OEE performance especially if the same or similar products are made at various sites.

A word of warning is that, as outlined in Chapter 1, OEE is an improvement driver and not a comparative performance measure and as such should not be compared between equipment either at a site or between sites. It is closing the gap between the Baseline and Ideal Vision that is important, not some arbitrary OEE figure. If comparison is on the agenda, we would suggest that Production Efficiency (PE) be used rather than OEE, recognizing that PE can give a false sense of achievement as Planned Downtime and Setup or Changeover Time is left out.

Developing an OEE Data Capture Model for your Production Area or Line

	Element	Loss	Code	Location	Type	Reason (Open Field)
OEE	Availability	Planned Downtime	Start-of-Shift Meeting Break Lunch CI Time			
		Setup or Changeover Downtime	Fill Change Size Change CIP			
		Unplanned Recorded Downtime		Filler Caper Labeler Packing Palletizing	Mechanical Electrical Material Production	Jam Trip Not to Spec Adjustment
	Rate	Reduced Speed		Filler Caper Labeler Packing Palletizing	Mechanical Electrical Material Production	
	Quality	Rejects & Rework	Reject Rework	Filler Caper Labeler Packing Palletizing	Mechanical Electrical Material Production	

Having a Type column is basically using a "root cause by remedy" approach, which can be very helpful provided it doesn't become a "blame game." This is where you diagnose each loss by "who will fix this." For example, a downtime reason of "jam at in-feed" can be better expressed as "Material: poor quality" or "Mechanical equipment: in-feed problem," as each of these will jam the in-feed, but the cause/remedy is radically different.

Once the OEE Data Capture Model has been developed for each line, there should ideally be resources in place at a site level and, if appropriate, at an enterprise level to govern and improve the information-design policies on an ongoing basis. This should include updating Product/SKU lists and especially ideal speeds.

When setting up your Codes and Locations, it is desirable to have feedback and input from your experienced Operators who will have the best knowledge of what downtime event has occurred.

Unfortunately, we have found some sites where they have rushed into automated loss data capture only to find that duration and location are captured by the system; however, the type is often debatable (Production blaming Maintenance and Maintenance blaming Production), and the reason entered by the Operators is missing or inaccurate, with often the first reason on the menu selection or drop box being the biggest because it is the quickest and easiest one to click.

It should be recognized that from a Root Cause Analysis perspective, the Location captured will more than likely be relating to the Point of Observation rather than the Point of Occurrence. For example, you record loss for product being underweight at the weigh scales (Point of Observation); however, the Root Cause may be a fault with the filler (Point of Occurrence).

As such, gathering location data has to be monitored as it can be very valuable to identify what part of the line is generating the most losses provided it is clear you are looking for the Point of Occurrence, which may be difficult to identify on the run when the focus is getting the line running again.

The Type can also be misleading of true Root Cause. For example, a Motor trips out, so it is an Electrical fault, but the root cause may be a Mechanical fault, causing the overload or a Production contamination problem requiring cleaning to free up a roller.

This is why getting the Operators involved in Root Cause Analysis in a timely manner (as soon as practical after the loss occurs) is the best way of understanding the actual situation. This is also why monitoring performance at least every hour by the Frontline Leader is so important so that they can ask the why questions while the information is still fresh in people's minds.

3. Reporting Capability

When it comes to reporting, many software packages have pre-canned reports. An alternative approach used by OFS has been to minimize this and instead provide an intelligence platform to help users "explore" for insight. The founder from OFS explained "the reason we did this, is in our original designs, we too had pre-canned reports but as we continued to expand our reporting to user requirements, we found we had over 150 reports and growing! So we substituted this for our analytics product where users now explore (and can create custom reports) themselves thus eliminating a dependency on OFS for creating new reports. As users are empowered to do this themselves, it also creates smarter users, although as a minor negative, the ramp-up time to get users there is a touch longer."

Another capability worth looking for is report sharing, including easy to export in a variety of formats.

4. Integration

Any software must easily take data in (e.g., schedule, product master, etc.) and export data out (e.g., Excel, feedback to SAP, or anything else such as the maintenance system etc.). This will create annoying limitations in the future if it is not considered early.

5. All-in-One versus Best-of-Breed

Many companies that have multisites have Enterprise Resource Planning systems such as SAP, JD Edwards, or similar, which is an all-in-one system. Using SAP as an example, apart from being a very popular fully integrated Enterprise Resource Planning system, it also has an OEE module, a scheduling module, a maintenance module, to name but a few; however, ask any SAP user and they will acknowledge that some of the modules are not Best-of-Breed. In other words, there are stand-alone modules in the marketplace, whether it be a CMMS (Computerized Maintenance Management System) or an OEE data capture system that is available and deemed by many users to be more user friendly and provide better outcomes. Sadly, most all-in-one systems only do one to two things really well, and everything else is poorly done, compared to the alternatives in the marketplace.

Another example we have seen is that some OEE data capture systems started life as scheduling software, which they do really well. They then expanded into OEE as an add-on, and it's OK, but not as good as the scheduling. A customer then buys OEE software that includes scheduling, believing it to be a shrewd purchase.

One of the best things with Best-of-Breed suppliers is that they come with passion and a team dedicated to propagating the one thing they do. This is usually not the case with All-in-One systems as they often cannot be the best at everything.

When it comes to choosing software, and making a choice between Best-of-Breed versus All-in-One, provided all compatibility issues are addressed, things to consider include the following:

- Best-of-Breed means consumer choice. You can choose a scheduling solution from vendor A, a maintenance solution from vendor B, and so on. It is like the way stereo components can now be from independent vendors, which wasn't always the case.
- All-in-One can mean limited choice and supplier dependency. Best-of-Breed must be made to integrate; it's the only way it can exist.

How Do We Ensure We Are Capturing the Right Information?

In "Photo 6.1a and b" above, it appears that the focus is to ensure that the OEE figure looks good for management rather than capturing the true loss situation. At this site, we observed the situation where the Operator running one machine was called away to assist another Operator on another nearby machine so as not to cause losses on that machine. This meant that the first machine was classified as "scheduled not to run" and hence no impact on OEE, while the other "problem" machine did not incur any OEE loss because the second Operator assisted

IF YOU SHUTTING ANY MACHINE BECAUSE OF NO MANNING OR ATTEND MEETING , OR STOP FOR MEAL BREAKS THEN CLASSIFY THIS DOWNTIME AS " SCHEDULED NOT TO RUN" THIS WAY YOUR MACHINE OEE WONT BE AFFECTED- SEE TEAM LEADER IF YOU NEED MORE CLARIFICATION.

(a)   (b)

Photo 6.1   (a) Data capture station on production line for Operator inputs. (b) Instructions posted above data capture station.

with keeping the machine running by reworking the product on the run, while the Operator was trying to get the adjustments right.

This example highlights the need to explain to Operators "why" OEE loss data is being captured rather than just how to do it. We have found that most Operators prefer their line or equipment to run perfectly and have quick and easy changeovers because it reduces their workload. Hence, if Operators understand that the OEE loss data is being used to identify all the problems that cause them frustration, so that the problems can be reduced or eliminated, they will be more focused on ensuring the correct loss information is collected, especially if they are involved in coming up with possible solutions to the losses and given regular feedback on the progress of improvements.

How Do We Want the Information Displayed/Accessed?

The information collected should be displayed in real time to the Operators responsible for OEE performance in a format that is visually easy to interpret and ideally where any deviations to standard are highlighted.

OEE performance is also one of the measures that Frontline Leaders should be monitoring at least hourly and reporting on at their Daily Review Meeting.

As such, the OEE Performance should be accessible ideally via a smartphone or tablet that can be carried by the Frontline Leaders (and their Supervisor and Manager). The information should also be in an easy-to-understand format structured to support continuous improvement.

Defining the Purpose of the Loss Data Capture System

Before selecting any system, you should first specify in sufficient detail exactly what you want it to achieve for you, and most importantly how you will use the information that is collected.

This should be supported with the following:

- Who will be entering the operating parameters for each product run?
- What are the criteria for identifying that a changeover or setup has been completed and who will make this decision (often once a new run commences there is "adjustment time" before the "required rate" is achieved)?
- Who will be entering the type of loss?
- Who will be entering the reason for the loss?
- Who will be entering the "point of observation" of the loss (recognizing the "point of occurrence" may be different and not found until a Root Cause Analysis is conducted)?
- Who will be reviewing the data **and why**?
- How will quality losses identified after the run be accounted for (1000 units are produced and then, say, 2 hours later, the Lab advises that 200 units need to be reworked or scrapped)?
- How will the information be displayed?
- Who will have access to the information?
- What trend reports can be generated and will they use SPC Upper and Lower Control limits to help in interpreting the results?
- How frequently will the data captured be used for improvement decision making?

Key Learnings from Chapter 6

- Don't Automate before Simplifying.
- Develop an OEE Data Capture Model outlining the main fields required before seeking to automate.
- Ensure that the right information is being captured as opposed to information that makes the performance look good.
- Ensure that the display of the information generated is user friendly and easily accessible to your Frontline Leaders who should be monitoring it on an hourly basis and reporting it at their Daily Review Meeting.
- Define the purpose of the OEE Loss Data Capture System before seeking one out.
- Automating OEE Data Capture is an important part of the improvement journey; however, if not well thought out and done properly, it may prove to be a waste of time and investment.

Appendix: OEE Improvement Rating

Understanding, Measuring, and Improving Overall Equipment Effectiveness (OEE) can be elusive for many sites. Everyone is too busy working around never-ending problems to have time to sit back and reflect on how OEE should be properly measured and improved, resulting in a lot of frustration for people as the production plant and equipment doesn't perform to its full potential.

Below is a simple 10-Requirement rating sheet that can be used to do a quick health check on your OEE Improvement process for a Production Area or Line. If you score below 50%, we would suggest there could be significant opportunity for improvement. Use your score as a baseline for your improvement activities, and then as you apply the learning from this book, monitor the improvement to your score to ensure that you are focusing on the right things that will lift capacity and reduce costs and frustrations while creating a safer workplace.

Site:	*Rating Legend*
Production Area or Line:	0—No evidence of activity or 0% 1—Attempted but limited results or 10%
Assessor:	2—Some evidence of activity or 25%
Date of Assessment:	3—Halfway to full implementation or 50% 4—Close to full implementation or 75%
	5—Fully implemented or 100%

Defined Production Area OEE Rating

Requirements for OEE Improvement	0	1	2	3	4	5
1. OEE calculations are based on definitions where there is a direct correlation to good output produced and OEE performance (if OEE increases by 5%, then 5% good output is produced in the same time, or the same good output is produced in 5% less time)						
2. OEE definitions are documented, understood by everyone, and used consistently in all calculations						
3. OEE is measured and reviewed at least hourly so that corrective actions can be initiated where required in a timely way						
4. All OEE losses are understood down to Second-Level Pareto for both Loss and Section, and the OEE Loss Analysis Spreadsheet is used at least annually to identify the type and number of teams for future improvement activities/cycles						
5. Continuous recording of losses, sampling observations, and high-level calculations are all used to develop the OEE Loss Analysis Spreadsheet						
6. The OEE gap between Baseline and Ideal Vision has improved by at least 50%						
7. OEE improvement has sustained or improved over the last 6 weeks						
8. OEE Weekly Run Charts shows clear tendency of continuous improvement of OEE						
9. Production improvement activities are directed toward improving OEE or Lead Time						
10. OEE improvement has been translated into at least 5% regular ongoing continuous improvement time for Operators through their regular (weekly) Production Area Based Team improvement activities (Clean for Inspection, Train for Inspection, Manage by Inspection)						
Number per Column:						
Multiply by:	0	1	2	3	4	5
Score per Column:						
Total/50:						
× 2	%					

Index

About the Author

Ross Kenneth Kennedy commenced his working career in 1970 at the Port Kembla Steelworks (12 years), followed by Cable Makers Australia (5 years), and David Brown Gear Industries (3 years). Over these 20 years, he gained hands-on manufacturing and operational experience covering maintenance (14 years), production, operations, and executive roles before moving into management consulting.

In 1985, Ross developed his passion for Lean Production following his involvement in the Value Added Management (JIT) initiative by the NSW Government. Ross quickly and effectively applied the new Lean principles and practices first at the CMA Foam Group Lullaby Bedding Factory while Factory Manager, then CMA's Cable Accessories Factory as Site Manager before moving to David Brown Gear Industries as Manufacturing Manager to establish and oversee the relocation of the company from Sydney to Wollongong to a new facility set up on Lean principles and practices.

In 1989, after the new facility was well established and recognized for its leading edge improvements based on Lean, Ross was invited to join the new JIT/Lean practice being established by the Manufacturing and Operations Group of Coopers & Lybrand's International Management Consulting Practice based in Sydney.

Over the next 5 years, Ross had the opportunity to work on major assignments with some of the firm's leading Lean practitioners from the United States, Canada, and the United Kingdom. It was also during this time that he first came across TPM (a critical missing link in the Lean tool kit) in 1990 when he led one of the first implementations of TPM in Australasia under the guidance of John Campbell who was Partner-in-Charge of Coopers & Lybrand's Global Centre for Maintenance Excellence based in Canada and author of the internationally recognized maintenance book *Uptime*.

In August 1994, Ross established his own consulting practice specializing in TPM. He organized and chaired Australasia's first TPM conference in 1995, and at the request of the delegates at the conference, Ross, with several colleagues, founded The Centre for TPM (Australasia) in January 1996 to provide a membership-based organization to support Australasian industry and academia.

After extensive research including a trip to Paris in 1997 to attend Europe's first World-Class Manufacturing & JIPM-TPM Conference and associated workshops with leading TPM practitioners from throughout the world, The Centre for TPM (Australasia) launched its TPM^3 methodology in January 1998, which is an enhanced and expanded Australasian version of the Japan Institute of Plant Maintenance (JIPM) Third-Generation TPM embracing the Toyota Production System and spanning the entire Supply Chain.

Since then, CTPM has been involved with a wide range of leading manufacturing, mining, processing, utilities, and service companies. For example, from September 1998 to June 2003, CTPM assisted Telstra in rolling out their TPM initiative to more than 200 teams servicing their Customer Access Copper Network in 16 Regions throughout Australia, resulting in more than $110 million in savings.

Ross has been actively involved with Lean Production since 1985, TPM since 1990, and Australasian TPM & Lean (TPM^3) since 1998 and has delivered publicly more than 200 workshops and papers on the subjects both within Australia and overseas.

CTPM, under the direction of Ross with his team of experienced CI Specialists, is presently assisting more than 30 sites located in Australia, New Zealand, Thailand, Indonesia, and China on their TPM & Lean/CI journeys to Operational Excellence and World Class Performance.